Fear no more the heat o' the sun,
Nor the furious winter's rages;
Thou thy worldly task has done,
Home art gone, and ta'en thy wages';
Golden lads and girls all must,
As chimney sweepers, come to dust.

       ❧ SHAKESPEARE

It is in regard to death that our condition is most shrouded in doubt. We are tormented not only by the pain and the gradual breaking up of the body but also, and even more, by the dread of ceasing to be. But a deep instinct leads us rightly to shrink from and to reject the utter ruin and total loss of the personality. Because we bear witness within ourselves the seed of eternity....

       ❧ VATICAN COUNCIL II

For
Jack van Bemmel

Third printing 2015

TWENTY-THIRD PUBLICATIONS
A Division of Bayard
One Montauk Avenue, Suite 200
New London, CT 06320
(860) 437-3012 or (800) 321-0411
www.23rdpublications.com

ISBN 978-1-58595-727-9
Library of Congress Catalog Card Number: 2008940045
Printed in the U.S.A.

Contents

Part Three: Appendices

Preface

This book is basically an anthology. It draws on excerpts from some of my previous books and adds to them some new material. The subject, of course, is funeral homilies and the preacher, especially if he or she has been at a parish for a long time, is constantly in need of fresh insights, a new slant on some very old Scripture.

Yet I have offered these funeral homilies—half of which have never been published—with some hesitation. The hesitation is due to the fact that funerals are so exquisitely personal. They necessarily abound with personal references, local color, inside knowledge and jokes. Reading these funeral homilies, then, might seem a bit like reading another's mail. So why did I include them? I did so because I am convinced that behind and beneath the very specific person and circumstances the reader does not know, lie a universal pattern and framework for another homilist's reworking. In other words, I feel that the creative homilist can extract the personal names and histories and discover a fundamental structure, an outline, a homiletic lead, a meaningful story on which to build his or her own thoughts and apply them to the here and now.

Introducing each homily will be a brief background of the type of person who is deceased. Such an introduction may guide another's thoughts. It is imperative, by the way, that one reads the Scripture reference along with the homily. Note that since these homilies were given over many years there is necessarily some repetition as the same stories and gospel paradigms are applied to different people.

Before I offer these homilies, however, there is a long excursion in Part I—skipped without guilt—into our contemporary social and religious context that impinges on how we handle funerals and how we preach. Things are not the same. People are not the same. Ethnic makeup is not the same. Religious practice and religious literacy are not the same. In short, the funerals of yesterday and the funerals of today are worlds apart, evolving from black-vested gloom to white-vested joy. Still, every funeral is a teachable moment as they say—the *Order of Christian Funerals* calling us "a teacher of faith and the minister of consolation"—and what is offered here is a way to make the most of it. For whether in gloom or glee we humans fear death and use all kinds of stratagems to deny it. Epitaphs once somber like this:

> *Remember man, as you walk by*
> *As you are now so once was I.*
> *As I am now, so shall you be,*
> *Remember this and follow me.*

Have given way to:

> *Here lies Johnny Yeast*
> *Pardon me for not rising.*

or

> *Here lies the body of Jonathan Blake.*
> *Stepped on the gas*
> *Instead of the brake.*

The soulful *Dies Irae* has given way to "On Eagles' Wings," the clergyman to a "Funeral Provider," the coffin to the urn, the traditional liturgy to media celebration. But, for all of this, grief remains, loss hurts, questions arise, tears flow, rituals, often outside the Church, spring up. How to be present, how the parish as a whole responds, is part of the implicit subtext on which rests the homily itself. So, first, a thumbnail sketch of the things that shape us today.

Part One

The Way We Are

The
Faithful Departed

Funerals, like all the sacramental celebrations, unavoidably take place within the current culture. So, to begin with, we take a look at today's social and their emotional landscape.

To begin with, there will be many strangers at our funerals, not only non-Catholics, but also those Catholics (the faithful departed) who compose the seventy percent of those who do not attend church regularly. They are drawn to the Eucharist twice a year as Andrew Greeley says, but, while still holding firm to their Catholic identity, they don't feel they'll go to hell for missing Mass. In any case, it's likely that they may not know Mass etiquette, responses, or songs, and that has to be kept in mind. All the way around, as James Davidson says, this generation "is less religious in childhood than their parents and grandparents; they report fewer experiences of God's presence in their lives; and they are less committed to the Church."

The recent Pew Forum on Religion and Public Life survey backs this up. It found that most Americans have a very non-dogmatic approach to faith, and they present an extraordinary amount of diversity. For example, ninety-two percent of Americans believe in God but only seventy-one percent are absolutely certain of this belief. Of those who do believe in God sixty percent say God is a person while a quarter say that, no he is an impersonal force. More than half of Americans say religion is very important to them but seventy percent don't believe their faith tradition is the sole path to salvation. On the contrary, even for Catholics, to think there is only one exclusive way to salvation simply doesn't compute. It sounds undemocratic and elitist to the extreme. Father Edward Hayes, that wonderful author on spirituality, is an exponent of this common attitude:

> Religion is like a great towering Sequoia. Its roots go down into the subterranean prehistoric, pre-temple times, and after centuries its trunk has grown up thick, tall and sprouting countless branches, all of which reach upward to the heavens—to God. Each branch is unique and a living extension of the great tree. There are those who may find this last statement offensive, since they have been taught that their particular religion isn't just a branch, it is the tree....
>
> The various denominations within Christianity, along with the great religions of the world, all love and worship the one, same God. The God whom Muslims or Jews or Christians or any other peoples worship is the same God you worship. The names and images of God may vary richly, but the God who is named and praised in prayer is the one same Divine Mystery.
>
> "Companions on the Journey," in Sacred Journey,
August/September 2008

Added to this "many paths to the same God" motif, sixty-eight percent in the Pew study believe that there is also more than one way to interpret the teachings of their own faith. Furthermore the majority of Catholics and Protestants say their churches should adjust traditional practices to new circumstances or adopt modern beliefs. Most religious Americans (again, this strongly includes Catholics) believe they have to make up their own minds no matter what their religious authorities may teach. The ultimate arbiter of belief and morals is their own consciences—often minus the critical adjective "informed." Catholics, for example, may like the pope and cheer him on when he comes to visit and they're quite glad to have him as a unifying figure, but they do not feel compelled to accept everything he teaches.

It comes as no surprise to learn that Americans tend to be quite suspicious of all religious authority anyway, and, therefore, ties to the institutional church are weak. This explains why Catholic marriages have not only plummeted but also why the majority of Catholics believe they can be good Catholics and not be married or buried in the Church. In short, at every funeral there is a spread of the old devout and the younger seekers, both of whom must be reminded to turn off their cell phones. Finally, it has been often noted that there are more ex-Catholics than Presbyterians. A lot leave because of mixed marriages, others because of run-ins with pastors, disagreements, the clergy abuse scandal, or simply from indifference as each generation bequeaths a thinning Catholicism to the next. The point is that with such a social context a funeral can be a subversive invitation to return. It definitely falls into the category of a teachable moment.

The Demographics

Something we should all be aware of is the rapidly changing ethnic composition of the United States. Barring some catastrophe such as famine or earthquake or pestilence, today's ethnic minorities will constitute the majority in about two generations from now. Think of that. Asians, Hispanics, blacks, and others will predominate. Mostly this is due to the higher birthrates of these groups and the fact that more and more current American women, especially as they gather advanced degrees, are not having children at all. In any case, these ethnic groups are religiously and culturally conservative and socially liberal and as they become the majority, they bring with them traditions and expectations that will or should influence the Church's liturgies and devotional life. They are biblical not speculative like us. They resonate with traditional Catholic identity especially those that are Marian inspired. Religion is highly important to these folk of the southern hemisphere, the Church's new center of gravity. We have to speak to them in a different voice from that of middle class white European Americans. In this regard we would be wise to retrieve much of the folkloric Catholicism we jettisoned after Vatican II.

We have to recall that in our not-too-distant past, our European immigrant forebears sent their kids to parochial schools, jealously preserved their national customs, faithfully attended novenas and missions, held processions, ate ethnic foods blessed by the priest, wore crucifixes and medals, prayed to patron saints, and built shrines in their houses. There was, in short, a complex network of ethnic identity and neighborhood community mixed in with faith and Church. Nationality, customs, public rituals, and religious practices were one, and this created a fundamental cohesive force for the Church. To this degree the Church lived in the culture but was not a part of it. This marriage of religion, ritual, and ethnicity, this mutual interpenetration of social and religious life, this easily lived identity of culture and faith is what we call "thick" Catholicism, and it formed a cocoon of institutions, beliefs, and practice. The staples of the faith—the requirement of fasting from midnight, a strict Lent, the ember days, fish on Fridays, the cult of the saints, parish missions, the habits of the nuns, the cassocks of the priests, incense, miraculous medals, novenas, sodalities, weekly or monthly confession, the Latin Mass, the Angelus, first Fridays—all blended into the rhythm of the liturgical year. Someone once described the old texture of Catholicism this way:

> The Catholic Church of yesterday had a texture to it, a feel: the smudge of ashes on your forehead on Ash Wednesday, the cool candle against your throat on St. Blaise's day, the waferlike sensation on your tongue in Communion. It had a look: the oddly elegant sight of the silky vestments on the back of the priest as he went about his mysterious rites facing the sanctuary wall in the parish church; the monstrance with its solar radial brilliance surrounding the stark white host of the tabernacle; the indelible impression of the blue-and-white virgin and the shocking red image of the Sacred Heart. It even had a smell, an odor: the pungent incense, the extinguished candles with their beeswax aroma floating ceilingward and filling your nostrils, the smell of olive oil and sacramental balm. It had the taste of fish on Fridays and unleavened bread and hot cross buns. It had the sound

of unearthly Gregorian chant and the *Flextamus genua* and the mournful *Dies Irae*. The Church had a way of capturing all of your senses, keeping your senses and your being enthralled.

Everybody knew who was a Catholic, including the Catholics themselves. Their language gave them away. Who else went around talking about "serving Mass," or using words like "transubstantiation" or "contrition" or "the occasions of sin"? Who else crossed themselves when passing a church or didn't eat meat on Friday? Catholicism had a coherent philosophy and respected writers. Catholics even gained some measure of respect with their vocal anti-Communism, the appearance of popular public figures like Bishop Fulton Sheen and Thomas Merton, and the popularity of blockbuster movies like *Going My Way, The Bells of St. Mary's, Come to the Stable, On the Waterfront*, and others that gave a favorable face to the Church and clergy. The old mantra, "Catholics can't be Americans," went underground during World War II when so many American Catholics entered the service.

Mainstreaming

Gradually, the ethnic neighborhoods, the "glue" that provided for a "thick" Catholicism, disappeared. After World War II, the GI bill allowed Catholics, for the first time, to enter secular colleges and move into the professional mainstream. People escaped to the suburbs in the '30s, '40s, and '50s, which, long before Vatican II, had a powerful effect on breaking down Catholic identity and community. Through universal education and the media, the grandchildren of the European immigrants were homogenized into secular "Americans" who no longer spoke the language, kept the customs, or went to church—in fact, they were embarrassed by these things—and who coveted designer labels and got divorced like everyone else. In fact, Catholics fell all over themselves to be just like any other middle class, affluent Americans. Thus corporate capitalism, deconstructing education, upward mobility, the suburbs, prosperity, and an endless menu of adventuresome and exciting "extreme realities" have moved Catholics, who no longer clustered around their parish churches—boring by comparison—into mainstream America.

The net result is that today, as every poll has shown, Catholics are indistinguishable from their fellow citizens in terms of ethical (media driven) values, social mores, and cultural tastes. The net result is a certain loss of identity, the loss of a specifically Catholic lore and ritual. So, how do they spend Holy Week? No longer fasting or attending services or making pilgrimages from church to church or taking the newly blessed Easter water home. No, school's out and even the best Catholics are at Disneyland.

Folkloric religion

Well, you can't go home again and I'm not advocating the surrender of genuine progress but perhaps it's time to recall and upgrade some of the sensuous devotions and artifacts of Catholicism (purified of their sometimes near superstition and insular tendencies), build on their genius for ritual and song, and get serious about the doctrine of the Communion of Saints. It is noteworthy that another recent poll found that, in a ratio of 2 to 1, young adults preferred the old style churches to the new ones. The old churches were redolent with windowed and sculptured saints, vaulted ceilings that pointed beyond, music that was apart from the culture, a sanctuary that, like the Ark of the Covenant, housed the Sacred. The Quaker, computer-like character of some modern churches could pass for corporate headquarters. The overemphasis on the worshiping community ("Christ is present in the people, you know") short-circuits the movement toward transcendence. And people are looking for that.

What I am saying is that, given the fact that the Catholic Church in America is numerically free-falling and is only saved from hitting bottom by the influx of Hispanics, we ought to marry our religious culture to theirs. Our Evangelical brethren who have captured many of our Catholic Hispanics by shamelessly promoting our Lady of Guadalupe, a posture that would have horrified their Mary-hating ancestors, at least know where the contact points are. Even now every parish should have one Hispanic hymn on Sundays. People who in the past had no trouble singing *Adeste Fideles, Tantum Ergo* and *O Salutaris Hostia* can easily learn a phonetic Spanish hymn. Some missalettes already put out English-Spanish editions. A shrine or statue to our Lady of Guadalupe should substitute for one of the many other Marian depictions.

Well, all this commentary seems a long way from the subject of funerals. But my point is that, with a someday majority Hispanic presence, a parish ought to creatively revive fitting devotions, music and art that overflow to the funeral liturgy. Not to mention, as I have indicated, that even today's American young adults are quite open to the devotional life and are awash in ritual, albeit often a secular version. But they love ritual. Look how they dropped flowers, made collages, wrote songs when Princess Diana was killed. Look at their ritualistic songs and symbols, their obsessive sartorial "statements." We have to offer them something more than the Mass of the Resurrection.

The Arrangers

As high consumers Americans like to display status. It's not just mega-mansions and yachts but it's the freedom to create one's own image even if that image keeps on changing with every new fad or celebrity imitation. Those who wed a secular mindset to affluence now design their own non-religious Christmas holiday motifs (lest they offend some pluralist), their own birthday bashes, their own weddings, and now their own funerals. They have turned them from sacred moments to fun celebrations. The ornate and exotic Christmas decorations, the average seventy thousand dollar wedding and now the festive funeral all require an expert, the Arranger. There are whole industries, readily accessed on the Web, that cater to these affairs, offering creative staging, politically correct invitations, a trained staff, and funky rituals.

Not only that but on certain Web sites these folks can even obtain state certificates conferring instant ordination to witness weddings and perform funerals. They can register, for example, at a certain Web site in Pennsylvania whose credo is "Each person's spirituality has to be developed individually. Everyone is free to draw upon whatever religious tradition and behaviors are most appropriate for their own unique situation and background." Perfect for a narcissistic, individualistic society! For forty bucks they're entitled to be called "reverend." Preacher mills (which are legal) can ordain as many as twenty million ministers a year. These online ministers populate the country with such online names as "The Church of Spiritual Humanism." That's why some are abandoning church rituals altogether and opting for the customized "happenings" they offer.

Finally, in these days of disappearing neighborhoods, anonymous living, and high mobility, you don't even have to be present physically. You can offer your virtual presence as you go online and electronically attend the wake and funeral services and interact with the bereaved. You can send an electronic condolence card.

The results of this high individualism are evident everywhere. Every pastor, for example, cringes at the bride and groom who want an *American Idol*-type wedding with a bevy of cameras to record every moment, flowers imported from Brazil, the bride dressed in denim, an entrance on the lawn from a helicopter, readings from Elton John and Marianne Williamson and music by The Who. The latest one I heard is from a man who told me that his niece was initially married in a church in Brooklyn. It wasn't her home parish but the borrowed church did have the long aisle she felt necessary for her proper on-camera entrance. The marriage lasted six months. She recently met someone else, flew everyone down to Aruba, and had a wedding ceremony on a topless beach with a New Age minister who told the bridal party to face the pristine water—sign of cosmic purification— and ignore the topless bathers. (He said it wasn't easy.)

The sad part is that in these sacred and fundamentally communal events the focus is so entirely individualistic. A secular source, "Miss Manners," speaks for us. She warns prospective brides and grooms that the wedding is not there to showcase themselves and that, despite the brainwashing by the wedding industry "your wedding is not about you. Your courtship is about you and your marriage will be about you. And unless you drag all your wedding guests off to an exotic destination, your wedding trip will be about you. But a wedding is about your public entrance into the civic and often religious rituals of the society. Its emotional strength comes from long continuity—knowing that you are repeating the steps of those who preceded you and those who will follow." Wise, very "Catholic" words but the fact is that a sense of communal responsibility, of being part of a wider picture, that one's actions, no matter how private, always resonate in the public square is beyond most people today. They've been too trained to "join an army of one."

I go on about this because it shows how much work we have to do and the need for the evangelization of Catholics. I go on about this because this is the mentality the family brings to the funeral planning where the same demand to "personalize" the funeral is evident. I am far from suggesting that we cave into these secular fads at a funeral. But I am saying that we should be aware of this media mentality and how much education we have to do. And surely we must shrink from offering any kind of bland ceremony or indifferent or canned homily. We are in a sense on trial. The church funeral is in its own right powerful enough, full of symbol and gesture as it is, and, as I said, is a teachable moment. Our best music, careful ritual, and meaningful homily must take advantage of that.

A Parish Reaches Out

"If one member suffers in the body of Christ which is the Church, all the members suffer with that member" (1 Cor 12:26). For this reason, those who are baptized into Christ and nourished at the same table of the Lord are responsible for one another...[thus] when a member of Christ's Body dies, the faithful are called to a ministry of consolation... to care for the dying, to pray for the dead, to comfort those who mourn.

Order of Christian Funerals

There are many creative things parishes around the country are doing to make the whole death-funeral experience humane and meaningful, and we should try to seek them out. What follows is but one parish's attempt to do this. Not everything is necessarily the best, but hopefully suggestive.

The Priest Shortage

Before we take a look at the suggestions on how a parish, as a total faith community might respond to the death of a parishioner, we want to detour and take a look at the Church's self-inflicted priest shortage. With so many of our parishioners living longer but also dying at around the same time, some parishes replete with senior citizens' developments—my home state of New Jersey, for example, has the second largest number of senior citizens after Florida—have lots of funerals. One parish in my diocese averages four funerals a week, over 200 a year! Since the same people, neighbors and friends from the development, tend to come all the time, what do you say after the hundredth funeral? What new homiletic word can you preach? And do parish priests really want to do funerals all the time? It's got to be depressing. And with the shortage of priests there's not much help available.

Some thoughts: First, for those who do not have strong affiliations or preferences, we may have to encourage having funeral *ceremonies* either in church or at home or at the funeral parlor (OCF #179) rather than the funeral Mass, pretty much the same as we offer a wedding ceremony rather than the Nuptial Mass. In our current book of rituals both wedding and funeral ceremonies can be quite lovely and meaningful. In fact the *Order of Christian Funerals* contains six rituals from the vigil service to a "Funeral Outside Mass" and specifically uses the wording "Funeral Liturgy" rather than "Funeral Mass" to underscore this. Again, this latter option is especially attractive for those who have only a marginal connection to the church. And with cremation so popular, it gives the survivors more flexibility as to when they might want a memorial service. Moreover, as in the wedding ceremony, a deacon can preside or even a lay minister. As the U.S. Bishops say, "As for the stations at home and at the cemetery, priests sometimes are unable to lead them because of a shortage of clergy...In view of these considerations, the faithful must be urged to recite the usual psalms and prayers themselves when there is no deacon or priest present." Perhaps there ought to be formally trained and commissioned lay ministers specifically to lead funerals. The funeral ceremony is on the books so it's really a matter of patiently and publicly educating the people about this option.

Second, there is the far-out suggestion that we have a corporate funeral Mass. That is, why not have one funeral Mass for all those who died in the past month? This is especially workable if all or most were cremated or buried in a separate ceremony. Yes, this suggestion is pretty offensive to an individualistic people who want "their"

Mass, and it would be a hard sell. But someday, with careful preparation and education, someone might suggest the custom of a communal funeral Mass. Anyway, let's turn to...

The Evolution of a Funeral Policy

Years ago, sparked by reading Jessica Mitford's book, *The American Way of Death,* and having long noted how costly and how commercialized and, yes, even how the faith dimension had almost drowned in the competitive trappings of American Bigger and Better, I consulted local funeral directors to see if we could make funerals simpler, more Christian, less expensive. They were quite cooperative.

In due time, after much consultation, I sent a letter to all parishioners discussing the Christian view of death and burial, and tentatively offering the following: (a) the parish policy on eligibility for Christian burial; (b) the encouragement towards simplicity by purchasing a simple wooden coffin; (c) the option of wakes in the church rather than in the funeral parlor; (d) a pre-death set of wishes and instructions; (e) a trained group of parishioners who would guide and assist the family (called the Lazarus Ministry). Let's take them one by one.

Who Gets Christian burial?

The church allows catechumens a Catholic funeral. So too for a child who dies before baptism or is stillborn or miscarried, presuming the parents intended to have the child baptized. Likewise it allows a Catholic funeral for a deceased baptized non-Catholic who might reasonably be presumed to desire or prefer a Catholic funeral. A non-Catholic spouse who attends Mass regularly with his or her family would be a good example. Consistently, non-Catholics may also be buried in a Catholic cemetery where his or her family members are buried.

It's the baptized Catholic who can hardly be considered exemplary who poses the pastoral problem. Some, like "notorious heretics" (canon 1184:1), are excluded, of course, although strangely, the Church allows for non-notorious heretics to be buried with a Catholic Mass "provided their own minister is not available" (canon 1183:3). But mostly, on the everyday parish level, we're in the realm of the just plain public sinners who have kept the Catholic label but who are hardly material for canonization. What do we do with them? Let me respond this by sharing a homily I once gave (and perhaps someone might adapt in preparation for a parish policy.) It's titled...

"Burying Ol' Blue Eyes"

On May 14, 1998 Ol' Blue Eyes, the Chairman of the Board, the leader of the Rat Pack, Francis Albert Sinatra, died. For fifty years he was a star. No one could wrap himself around a song like Frank Sinatra, the master of intimate popular singing. He was, as Frank Rich of the *New York Times* wrote, "one of the greatest artists of any kind this country has produced." But also, as Frank Rich added, "In death, though, it's abundantly clear that Sinatra creates a national problem for American sensibilities...[for] as a human being, he not infrequently resembled a thug."

We all know what happened. He went from the skinny Hoboken singer in the bow tie to the hard-drinking sophisticate who personified the new modern mood, which was, in the phrase of movie critic Stephen Holden, "the golden age of bad behavior without consequences." He hung around with mobsters from Lucky Luciano to Sam Giancana who shared Judith Exner with President Kennedy. He had those he disliked beat up or did it himself. He was vindictive and insulting, calling Barbara Walters "the ugliest broad on television" and getting one of his critics, the famed musicologist Jonathan Schwartz, fired from his job.

Committing public adultery with Ava Gardner while married to Nancy, marrying her and two more women, Frank Albert Sinatra can hardly be called an exemplary Catholic or any kind of a Catholic, even though, technically, his first marriage was annulled, his second and third marriages were declared invalid and his fourth marriage was validated in a private ceremony at St. Patrick's Cathedral in 1979. Yet, he *was* a Catholic for he met the standard sole minimal requirement for that position: He was baptized in the same Church as the pope. He died and people came from all over to see him. And that included the

Catholic Cardinal Archbishop of Los Angeles. And he, reprobate that he was, was given a Catholic burial with a Catholic Mass.

Some sneered. They said, "Money talks." How can they—"they" meaning the Cardinal, the Church as a whole—give a Catholic Mass to a very public sinner who was in his lifetime and in his conduct no more "Catholic" than the man in the moon? He did it his way, not the Catholic way. The next thing, says the cynic (usually Catholic), I suppose they'll give Ted Kennedy who is ill and Madonna, should she reconvert, a Catholic Mass when their times come.

They suppose right. And here is where we must rise above the knee-jerk reactions and tabloid thinking and pause as a Catholic community and ask why. Here we must listen, for our own personal spiritual benefit, to two reasons why Frances Albert Sinatra and his ilk were given a Catholic burial—and should have been.

The first reason can be found in the public parish policy that I as pastor voiced many years ago. In our annual parish manual it read: "With few extraordinary exceptions–and there must be some—everyone shall receive Christian burial. No one, no matter how poor or indifferent a Catholic, no matter how scandalously a person lived or died, whether naturally or by his own hand or another's, will be denied Christian burial. The gospel imperative is that when a person is dead, all is over, and the only final obligation the Christian community has in charity is to pray for the deceased and to demonstrate by its liturgy that wideness and kindness that Christ himself showed. For a Christian community to deny its ritual of prayer and worship to even a public sinner is not to imitate Our Master who prayed for those who crucified him."

What this policy is saying is that the focus is never on the deceased—whether saint or sinner—*but on the faith community* which takes to heart these words of Jesus: "You have heard that it was said, 'You shall love your neighbor but hate your enemy.' But *I* say to you, Love your enemies, *and pray for those who persecute you* so that you may be children of your Father in heaven; for he makes his sun rise on the evil and on the good and sends rain on the righteous and the unrighteous. For if you love those who love you, what reward do you have? Do not even the tax collectors do the same? And if you greet only your brothers and sisters, what more are you doing than others? Do not even the pagans do the same? Be perfect, therefore, as your heavenly Father is perfect" (Mt 5:43–48).

"Love your enemy and pray for those who persecute you." Frank Sinatra, like John F. Kennedy or Madonna *are* "enemies" in that they do not practice or uphold or exemplify Catholic life. In fact, they embarrass and shame us; they have persecuted us by their lifestyles and scandals. There's no denying that. But—and remember this—*they* are not the point. *We* are. Under the imperative imposed by Jesus in the words we just heard, we are to pray for those who persecute us. Therefore, giving Christian burial and a Mass to the unworthy and scandalous says nothing about them but everything about us and our obedience to Christ's words. Giving Christian burial to the unworthy does not endorse *their* life. It endorses *ours.*

Don't you see what's at stake here? Oh, I'm sure in this imperfect world that money and celebrity talk and the famous and infamous get what they want even in death, but, once more, they are not and never were the point. *We* are the point and how seriously we want to be disciples even to practicing the hard sayings of Jesus.

So, how come Frank Sinatra got a Catholic burial and Mass? Is it because money and fame talk loud? Some, as we said, will say that. They always do. But now you know better. He got a Catholic burial and Mass because *we* talk loud.

The Catholic burial and Mass says that, much as we would like to, we will not "hate the enemy," we will *not* love only those who love us, we will *not* greet only our brothers and sisters in the practice of the faith, but we will try hard to love our enemies and in our public liturgy pray for those of our own who have persecuted us. We refuse to let them determine who we are. The Catholic burial Mass for the scandalous is the faith community's living out of the gospel. It has, I repeat, nothing to do with them or their status as public sinners. It has everything to do with us and our status as public disciples.

There is, as I said before, a second reason for giving Catholic burial to those who were unworthy of the name. That reason is that publicly we dare not close off the Spirit or give any kind of public notice that we do. We dare not confine the Spirit or define the limits of what the Spirit can do. We dare not pronounce on the compassion and grace and the action of God. We are in no position to make the final judgment, and the giving of a Catholic burial ritually leaves the question open: the question of God's mercy which gives latecomers the same pay as the first comers.

As an example, in the Scriptures, you might remember, young Stephen is stoned to death, a painful and horrible way to die. Another young man named Saul is there, wickedly approving and holding the coats of the stone-throwers to make their dreadful task easier. Saul did a shameful thing and Stephen's mother publicly cursed him. Yet that wicked young man, Saul, became, as we know, St. Paul. Stephen's mother wrote him off—we can understand that—but not God. The Spirit went beyond the limits of her grief and shock in a way she never imagined—nor he.

On Calvary a despicable young man, who admitted to terrible deeds and to getting what he deserved, was promised Paradise at the last minute. His was a last minute deathbed conversion known only to him and Jesus—that conversion, in my guess, being the result of years and years of his parents' tears and prayers. The publican and Prodigal Son of the parables, the woman caught in adultery, Peter, the Samaritan woman at the well, and Zacchaeus the tax collector of the gospels, Augustine, Ignatius, Malcolm Muggeridge, Tom Merton, and Dorothy Day of history—all are testimony to the fact that we never have the last word but God does. Granting a Catholic burial Mass to the seemingly unworthy says that we don't know what happened in the secrets of the heart at the last moment.

We are in no position to judge. We have no right to weigh what went on between the divine God and the human heart of a wretched sinner. The Mass of Christian burial for the public sinner simply proclaims the faith community's humility before this issue and its refusal either to dictate to or to second-guess the Spirit. In other words, the Catholic service proclaims the sovereignty of God, the everlasting possibility of a mercy we are not privy to.

So, there we are. Frances Albert Sinatra and many before him and many to come after him, with few exceptions—and there must be exceptions for heinous crimes, for the very worst cases—will be given Christian burial in the Catholic Church—not because of *their* disgraced position, but because of our graced position, a position derived from Jesus himself: our obligation to publicly pray for our very own who have persecuted us, our obligation to allow the Good Thief scenario its full play.

And so, to put it briefly, we must realize that the question never is for believers—even though we'll get asked it—what Frank Sinatra or any of his kind are all about that they got Christian burial.

It's the wrong question. The right question, remind your interrogators, is always, in these situations, what are *we* all about?

The parish policy quoted in the homily was distributed in our annual parish booklet along with our policies on all the sacraments. It errs, if you will, on the side of compassion and forestalls scandal.

Related Issues

Coffins

So often guilt plays a big part in coffin selection. One wants to do the best for one's loved one. If the relationship has been strained, an expensive coffin is a peace offering. Anyway, a "cheap" coffin sends a bad message to our status-conscious society. And so we add to our mounting bills by going all out. Some less than forthright funeral directors place the cheap coffin next to the Cadillac model in the showroom with the unspoken message, "Surely you love your mother enough to give her the very best." The simple wooden coffin cuts through all that. Its pedigree is strong. Recall the simple wooden coffins in which the last three popes were buried. Someone just has to start the trend. There have to be local carpenters who can make such a coffin. I came across a news item from the *Washington Post* telling how the children of a certain George Kramer, a building contractor, at his wish, built a simple pine box coffin for him. As his children said, "We're a family of carpenters. There's no reason we couldn't do this." Despite the sadness in doing the project, the children reported a certain peace and admitted that the work soothed them.

The Trappist Monks of New Melleray Abbey in Peosta, Iowa (888-433-6934) have taken as their ministry the production of wood caskets. You can order caskets from them as needed or pre-select a casket beforehand, paying now and having it delivered when needed. They range from $1,000 to $2,000. For the serious Catholic the simple wooden casket makes a faith statement that God has the last word.

Wakes in Church

When I first suggested wakes in the church the funeral directors around me were very supportive. They thought it was a good Catholic idea. There were a few, however, who, fearing somehow for lost revenue, were against it. They thought they were being pushed aside although that was not the intent. A delegation of them came to see me to talk me out of it. They raised all kinds of objections ranging from, "What if the body fell out of the coffin?" (Pick it up) to the clincher, "What if you're having Bingo in the hall? [attached to the church building behind the sanctuary] The response was that, although we really are Catholic we do not have Bingo. It went on and on until one of them, visibly agitated, stood up and told me that if I persisted with this idea of wakes in the church, when it came my turn to die, no one would bury me! I replied that when I died I had a great deal of faith in the local Board of Health and sooner or later someone would come and sweep me up.

As it turned out, their fears were groundless. They still handled the body from beginning to end and, instead of standing around the funeral parlor, they stood around the church.

Having the wake in church, especially for faithful Catholics, proved to be a powerful sign. The wake service was in a proper setting. Hospitality was in the parish hall. The Lazarus Ministry, as we shall see, provided care and direction at every turn. It was a real community celebration from beginning to end in the parish church.

The next morning we had the Mass of Christian Burial. Our policy was that, with few exceptions, the funerals were held at the usual daily community Mass (9 AM). The advantages were many. First, as the only priest in the parish, I didn't have to celebrate extra Masses. Second, the large consistent morning crowd provided the body English and clues to visitors and the occasional non-practicing Catholic who had no sense of church etiquette. The regulars, as usual, were the lectors and cantors (if family members or friends of the deceased did not do the job) and made the forceful responses. Third, they provided community. There is nothing more disheartening then to have eight people in a church that holds 600 or 700.

There is, by the way, no conflict with the current day's Mass intention. That intention is honored, even though there is a funeral. Obviously this funeral-at-the-community Mass works only if you have a normal amount of funerals, maybe one every few weeks or month. Too many funerals would subvert the daily community Mass. But, between non-church services at the funeral parlor and memorial services in our chapel in our Spiritual Center it was no problem. Finally, I might mention that it might be more people-friendly to have the funeral Mass or ceremony in the evening when workers can attend.

Pre-Planning

Because of our denial of death we don't talk about it much less plan for it. Many Catholics do not consider what they would want for their funeral and the family is often caught off guard as to what they should do or the details of the ritual. It becomes compounded when it's a case of non-practicing Catholics who, nevertheless, expect the parish to be there for them. These days, of course, you can go online to one of the many Web sites that have sprung up and use their services to customize your funeral and even join a club that swaps ideas. But long before the technological explosion we had sent papers to our parishioners on Living Wills and Pre-planned funerals. The people did not have to use these papers and were advised to consult their lawyers, but for those who wanted to, they could fill out these papers, keep copies for themselves and send a copy to the church where we put them on file. Many did and it proved very helpful. I am just including one paper here by way of example. The rest are in the Appendix. Many use professional planners.

Still, for all of this, the words of poet-undertaker, Tom Lynch, are worth pondering:

> Planning for funerals is no bad thing. And putting money aside for such things is sensible. But the planning is better done between husbands and wives, parents and children, friends and fellow pilgrims than between buyers and the sellers of things. Once we get the essentials right, the acces-

sories will take care of themselves. Have faith in people—they'll know what to do.

A good funeral is not a great investment; it is an existential moment in a family's history. It is not a hedge against inflation; it is a rite of passage. It is not a retail event; it is an effort to make sense of our mortality. It is not an exercise in salesmanship; it is an exercise in humanity.

Suggested Living Will

Copies to: _____

_____

In the event of a terminal illness and/or any condition where I am diagnosed as brain dead, I instruct you as follows:

1. At a certain moment, a doctor will determine that my brain has ceased to function and that, for all intents and purposes, my life has stopped. When that happens, do not attempt to instill artificial life into my body by the use of a machine or other extraordinary means. Do not call this my "deathbed." Call it my "Bed of Life," and let my body be taken from it to help others lead fuller lives.

2. Give my sight to a person who has never seen a sunrise, a baby's face, or love in the eyes of another.

3. Give my heart to a person whose own heart has caused nothing but endless days of pain.

4. Give my blood to a person who has been pulled from a wreckage of a car, so that she might live to see grandchildren at play.

5. Give my kidneys to one who depends on a machine to exist from week to week.

6. Take my bones, every muscle, every fiber in my body and find a way to make a crippled person walk.

7. Explore every corner of my brain. Take my cells, if necessary,

and let them grow so that some day a speechless person will shout at the crack of a bat and a deaf person will hear the sound of rain against the windows.

8. Give my soul to God.

9. If you must bury something, let it be my faults, my weaknesses, and all my prejudices against my fellow humans.

10. If by chance you wish to remember me, do it with a kind deed or word to someone who needs you. If you do all this that I ask, I will live forever.

Date: _____ Signed: _____

The Lazarus Ministry

There are many names for this ministry. This is ours. It's based on the premise that the funeral should not be the domain of only one person, the parish priest, but that the funeral is a part of the parish's overall pastoral outreach to the poor, the sick, the dying, and the bereaved. On the contrary, the whole community should be involved at least, for many, in an awareness of who has died and what's going on and how we are all connected.

As in all ministries I am strongly (vehemently?) insistent that they be grounded in (a) good theology, (b) competence, and (c) spirituality. People must know not only what they are doing but why, and how their gifts fit into the larger community. In short, good will is not enough. So when we began this particular ministry I solicited some people of the parish and began training them in the ways of Christian beliefs, funeral liturgy, and grief counseling. It took a long time. Since I am quite limited I called in the experts. We used the late Msgr. Joe Champlin's books and tapes (Ave Maria Press), the new rite of funerals, and other materials. I also solicited help and instruction from some hospice people from a nearby hospital, raided the local community college, and brought in some experts from New York. We heard tapes and speakers, discussed books and practicalities. We prayed and went on days of recollection. I wanted a strong foundation not only because I wanted the ministry to last but also because, as is my custom, when I stepped back, I wanted the members to be able to train others.

Perhaps the best way to understand what they do is to review what actually happens in the parish—actually what happens in most places.

A call comes to the office from the family or, more likely, the funeral director, to arrange for a funeral. As soon as the parish secretary gets the call, she immediately contacts the captain of one of the two Lazarus teams. That captain swings into action by calling the funeral director or family to see if they can meet quickly. The captain then gathers some members and they go to the grieving family's house. They bring with them two booklets: *Through Death to Life: Preparing to Celebrate the Funeral Rite* by Joe Champlin (Notre Dame, IN: Ave Maria Press, 1990) and our own homemade booklet entitled "Prayers, Readings, Hymns for the Communal Celebration of the Christian Wake Service and Mass of Christian Burial." The title is an exact description of its contents with the addition of a section of "Some Private Prayers and Reflections," the Prayers at the Cemetery, and, on the inside back cover, a summary of the funeral: time, date, celebrant, pall bearers, readers, etc. The family will ultimately receive it as a memento.

The usual questions are asked. What was this person like? What are your memories? (Information much needed by the homilist.) Had the deceased any requests concerning his or her funeral? Any special gifts to be brought up at the offertory that are meaningful (a photo, tool, craft, etc.)? Who will bring up the gifts? Does anyone want to do the reading? Will there be a eulogy? If so, it will be given at the wake service, not the Mass (more of this below). What hymns from the booklet? What readings? The Lazarus ministers go even further. They will offer practical helps such as babysitters, drivers, and pick-ups for those coming by plane, train, or bus. They will provide, if necessary, a luncheon or coffee and cookies after the funeral. This whole process and dialogue at the home itself, sitting around the kitchen table, is very therapeutic and comforting.

If the wake is at the funeral parlor, the Lazarus ministers will conduct it there. If in the church, some members are on hand when the
body is brought in.

They say:

> We welcome the body of our sister/brother,
> into this church,
> this community of believers. We mourn
> the loss but rejoice in his (her) return to the Father.
> Let us join together in the prayer our
> brother Jesus left us:
> (All recite the Our Father.)
> May his (her) soul and all the souls of
> the faithful departed rest in peace. Amen.

The Lazarus Ministry has meanwhile contacted others to drop off
cake and similar light refreshment for the church wake service. They
put on the coffee in the connecting parish hall and stay all during the
wake both in church and in the hall offering comfort, presence, and
hospitality. When the wake is over, the coffin is closed (if it had been
open) and the body remains in the church all night. The funeral director comes early to reopen the coffin and make any other preparations
before the family and friends arrive for Mass.

It is to be noted that our homemade booklets described above are
distributed throughout the church. At the end, before the body is removed, as is our custom, we invite the congregation to extend their
right hands as we sing the "Blessing of Aaron." As I mentioned, if
needed, we provide luncheon in the hall after the cemetery services.

Compassionate touches

We have found the following touches very helpful. The homily is
always taped and later given to the survivors. It's a great comfort
for family members and friends to gather at a later date and hear
the words again at an emotionally slower pace. When the Lazarus
ministers were at the home of the family they asked for a photo
of the deceased. This photo is now attached to a bulletin board in

church along with name and the date of death and burial information so that all parishioners have a chance to identify the deceased.
We all have the experience of not putting a name and face together
until we see them united. Underneath the bulletin board showing
the photo is a shelf on which rests the lovely "Book of the Dead"
(We got ours from Liturgy Training Publications). One of our gifted
calligraphers inscribes the name of the deceased in it. The book remains as a permanent feature in church so people can look through
its pages.

At Christmas we send a personal letter and a poinsettia to the
widow (widower) offering sympathy at this difficult time and on the
anniversary we send a printed card that reads:

> *With Sympathy and Love*
>   *It was a year ago that you lost someone near and dear
> to you. On this anniversary we, the people of St. Mary's
> parish, want to renew the promise of our prayers, the sym-
> pathy of hearts, and the fellowship of our common journey,
> united as we are, past, present and yet to come.*
>   *The people of St. Mary's*

Like most parishes we have a fine Bereavement Ministry ready to
help.

The all purpose card

Finally, the parish offered a "non-religious" card. Most people are familiar with the typical Mass cards for the deceased and we offered
them. But there are people, many non-Catholics (and Catholics) who
don't resonate with Mass cards and yet, at the same time, are very
open to charitable donations in memory of the deceased. The people
simply gave a donation to "St. Mary's Social Concerns Fund." The
money went directly to this ministry into its own bank account. The
parish never saw or touched this money. Happily this card proved
to be so popular that the Social Concerns was able to meet most of
its budget this way. The card is a simple foldover. On the front page
is the title St. Mary's Social Concern Fund with clip art depicting

someone dropping a coin into a poor box. On the inside front page are scriptural words from the epistle of St. James.

> *What good is it, my brothers, if someone claims to have faith but has no deeds? Suppose a brother or sister is without clothes and daily food, If one of you says to him, "Go, I wish you well; keep warm and well fed" but does nothing about his physical needs, what good is it? In the same way, faith by itself, if it is not accompanied by action, is dead.*
>
> James 2:14–17

On the inside of the second page is this inscription:

A Donation to
St. Mary's Social Concerns Fund
has been made on behalf of

_____

so that many people may continue to
receive the assistance they need.
This donation has been made by

_____

On the outside of this second (back) page are a

Partial List of Social Concerns Causes:

rent	rehab
utilities	placements
car repairs	medicine
counseling	Mercy Center
Martin House	Discovery House
Interfaith Neighbors	Birthright
food baskets	shut-ins
clothing	Endeavor House
heating	

This parish card was used on many other occasions, of course. It proved, as I indicated, to be very popular.

Summary

1. The Lazarus Ministry is very fruitful and fulfilling. To start one:
   a. Prepare the people by a letter; preach about it
   b. Have a written policy concerning those entitled to Christian burial
   c. If possible, celebrate the funeral at the daily community Mass
   d. Have a policy concerning flowers
   e. Offer an alternate card, socially based, to the Mass card.

2. The process is as follows:
   a. The Lazarus members visit the house on learning of a death
   b. They bring a booklet from which to choose music and readings
   c. They offer options for 1) preparation gifts, 2) readers, 3) eulogists
   d. They offer babysitting, drivers, and hospitality
   e. They contact the organist and funeral director to see where the wake is being held: at the funeral parlor or the church
   f. They welcome the body into church if the wake is there
   g. They do the wake service in either place
   h. They offer hospitality (refreshments, presence) if the wake is in church.

3. Follow-up consists of:
   a. A gift of the taped homily
   b. The exposition of a photo of the deceased in church
   c. A letter of sympathy at Christmas
   d. An anniversary card from the parish
   e. Inscription into the "Book of the Dead"
   f. The offerings of our Bereavement Ministry.

The Eulogy

January of 2003, Archbishop John J. Myers of Newark, New Jersey, banned eulogies, a fairly recent Catholic trend that popped up with the *Order of Christian Funerals*, during funeral Masses. It created quite a stir. It was too broad because there will always be pressure from some very high-profile families to have someone of prominence speak at the end. And once you cave in and make the exception you create the usual scandal that "money talks." The better approach is to consistently and patiently discourage eulogies at funeral Masses. Some indeed are splendid but more often they range from the trite to the trivial, not to mention falling captive to the speaker's irresistible tendency to talk too long. Eulogies celebrating the deceased's drinking binges, shady deals or "way with the girls" are not helpful. Tearful, maudlin, cloying words are embarrassing. Where the eulogy is permitted, many parishes limit it to five minutes and ask to see the text beforehand.

I don't like eulogies because they upstage the liturgy. You have a fine liturgy, appropriate readings, a thoughtful homily. You want to people to leave with the summary final blessings ringing in their hearts. It's a whole package, so to speak, the Church at its best. Then along comes a eulogy that reminisces about the past, tells funny stories, ends with a poem, and effectively erases all that went before and people leave with the last thing they heard. My own personal horror story is a funeral I had in another parish. After the rather meaningful liturgy was over, I sat down after the final prayer to give time to the eulogy or, I should say, the eulogies. First, one son came up and spoke for ten minutes. Then he was followed by little Timmy who came up to read a poem ("He's adorable!" wagged the heads in the pews to one another.) After adorable Timmy was finished, his sister, precious Megan, came up to sing a song. After precious Megan went off stage, a teenage nephew, not to be outdone, played "Danny Boy" on his saxophone. After him, another son came to share his thoughts for twenty minutes. The whole performance lasted longer than the entire funeral liturgy!

But by far the best solution, I think, is to encourage the eulogy at the wake service. It's often more informal, it allows others to pick up on memories and add to the words spoken and the context lends itself to such sharing. Eulogies belong at the wake service. It is worth noting that among the Hispanics the wake service is a very solemn ritual of death with certain prescribed rules (such as the Rosary) and where family members often stay with the body all night.

Cremation

Perhaps the biggest change in Catholic funerals is cremation. Rare in past times, it has become more and more common especially in transit urban areas. The Church, which hitherto forbade cremation, lifted its ban in 1963. "The Church earnestly recommends that the pious custom of burial be retained but it does not forbid cremation, unless this is chosen for reasons which are contrary to Christian teaching" (canon 1176:3). There's a history behind this last phrase. In December of 1869, the International Congress of Freemasons made it a duty for all its members to wipe out Catholicism. Cremation was proposed as one way to this end, since it was meant to undermine the faith of the people in the resurrection of the body. Anyway, at first the Church allowed cremation only *after* the body was present at the funeral Mass then later it allowed the cremation beforehand and the cremated remains could be brought into church in an urn.

Bishops are having second thoughts although I don't think they can stop the trend now. But they have a point when they note that Christianity is an embodied religion, an incarnational religion. It is the body that is baptized and filled with the Holy Spirit. It is the body that has worked, loved, and acted. It is Christ's body that has been raised up. The actual presence and burial of the human body better reflects this belief. My own thought is that cremation reflects too much the American love affair with industrial efficiency. It's too neat, quick, and disposable.

Allied with this is the observation of how burials in Catholic cemeteries have sharply declined over the decades. According to the Vatican people can now go elsewhere. People can now scatter the cremated remains to the four winds inadvertently shutting down the psychological need to have a place to visit and remember a loved one. The Church does not consider the scattering of ashes a reverent final disposition. (Burial at sea of cremated remains is a different story.) Nowadays cemeteries offer special plots for an urn or columbarium (niches in a mausoleum). But, as in so much else, individual choice prevails.

Waiting for a loved one to die, even with the ministrations of Hospice, is an excruciating process even for those of great faith. One friend of mine was clearly at a low point when she called me for comfort. A few days later I sent her this note:

Marge,

In our old Litany of the Saints—alas, seldom heard or chanted anymore—there is this perceptive cry: "From a sudden and unprovided death, deliver us, O Lord." It's a wonderful plea that for many, sadly, is not always answered. Tragedy, war, murder, accident, stroke, all can come like a thief in the night floating on a long distance telephone call.

While witnessing a Loved One's slow seeding into death and new life is painful, still, it's an answered incantation. There is a chance, denied to many, to say I love you many times over, a chance to gather family and friends, a chance to recall old memories and make new ones, a chance to repair and forgive, to put things and values in order.

Marge, life is always and everywhere a gift, a gift freely given and it should be freely given back. I suggest that you take these Advent-type days of awaiting Joe's rebirth to pray the prayer, "Lord God, I thank you for the gift of Joe's life. I now offer it back, thirty, sixty, hundredfold."

It's time for that prayer, Marge, and, I assure you, it is magnified countless times over in the prayers of those who love you and Joe.

Peace,

Part Two

The Funeral Homilies

"It's All Right"

(MARK 16:1–8)

This is the only generic funeral homily in this book. The homilist can personalize it.

"Will anyone remember?" I thought to myself. "But what if they do?"

Not too long ago a Soviet satellite with an atomic reactor aboard got into trouble and disintegrated over Canada, then fell to earth. I remember the fears of both the Soviets and the North Americans because of panic and because of the danger to health. Reading about that sort of thing reminds us that not too far underneath the surface all of us live with a great deal of fear. The fear of atomic hardware falling out of the sky.

And the everyday fears: the fear of losing our jobs; the fear of losing our health; the fear of losing our life's savings; the fear of another war; the fear of accidents; the fear of misfortune coming to our husbands, our wives, our parents, our children; the fear of being rejected, being unwanted; the fear of growing old and dependent, of being left alone without friends or family or loved ones. And finally, of course, there is the fear of loss: the loss of our faculties, the loss of our hearing, the loss of our mobility, the loss of memory, the loss of our loved ones, and the loss that we call death.

Even after we suffer these losses, particularly the loss of death, then there are other fears that creep in, fears we don't always express: the fear of losing control. Why couldn't I have done more? The fear of admitting our feelings of anger against God especially in suffering and death of innocent ones. If there is a God, why can't that God prevent babies from dying, or people from having cancer, or war or pestilence or hunger or famine, and all the other ills we suffer?

We want to shake our fist at God. We want to yell and scream and get terribly annoyed with God. And then sometimes after that there's a fear of a weak faith. "What kind of faith do I have? It's all right when I talk to others, but when it hits home, can I come to terms with all of these realities?"

It is all these kinds of fears that like so many mountains fall upon us, and like the people in our gospel, faced with the huge, great stone covering the tomb, they say, "Who's going to lift the stone?"

God says, "I will." Because from the fear of being unwanted or unloved, from the fear of death and all its anxieties, from the fear that there's no more to life than a bunch of molecules and ashes left over, God says through the prophets, "Tell the people: 'Behold, I have loved them with an everlasting love.'" And through Isaiah the prophet, God says, "Tell the people: 'Is it possible for a mother to forget the child of her womb? And even if it were possible that a mother could forget her own child, I shall not forget thee.'"

So it is God who is the one who will lift our fears, and we must believe in that. One of the greatest teachers of this century was the great philosopher and theologian Karl Barth; and in his old age, as people are wont to do, someone asked him what was the most important truth that he had learned in all of his vast study and thinking. And Karl Barth answered by quoting that old Protestant hymn that he learned in childhood. He said, "It's all in these words: 'Jesus loves me, this I know.'" And that was the conviction of decades of learning and studying; and he believed that.

You see the whole point of faith is that when we are met with this fear of darkness and death, we are not ashamed to call out, because the whole point of believing is the conviction that there is someone there to answer. It's what you parents have experienced when your children were very small and the lights went out at night and they got scared—those little back-up night lights were all right, but they were a short-term solution. The only way the children's fears could possibly be allayed was for mommy and daddy to go in and soothe the children, and pat them on the head, and soothe away the bad dreams, and tuck them in bed all over again, and give them those famous centuries-old words of reassurance, "Now, now, it's all right, it's all right."

And the secret of allaying those fears is, of course, love. It is the love of the mother and the love of the father that eventually still the children's worst anxieties, and put them back into that sleep of innocent peace.

It's the same way with us: When we are faced with this great anxiety called death, we tend to run the whole gamut of acceptance to anger, to disbelief, to hurt, to bewilderment, because after all, in death we always lose a person. But we have to remember that we never lose our relationship to God. We still have someone who says, *"It's all right."* That someone is God: God present in his word, in the Spirit, and in the church.

And it is in all these ways that God pats us on the head, and tucks us back into bed, and says, "Even though you have fears and anxieties, *it's all right."* Jesus made it all right, because it's this kind of love that burst the bonds of death. It is the kind of love that Jesus had that simply took away death's final word and made God's comfort the final word—instead of the grave. And this is what we must believe. Jesus said in the gospel, "Do not fear, little flock. It has pleased the Father to give you the Kingdom."

That's what we celebrate at a liturgy like this. Many of you are old hands at liturgies like this. You know well enough why we sing "Alleluia" as we enter the church. We sing that "Alleluia" because through our tears we believe that God has made it "all right" for the person who has died.

We wear the white vestments and put out bright flowers, not because we're insensitive to human grief, but it's our limited way of saying, *"Now, now, it will be all right."* We cover the dark coffin with the white cloth of the dead person's baptismal innocence because that's the way of saying, *"It's all right."* We bring the body and put it in front of the baptismal font beneath the crucified Savior because John says that out of Jesus' side flowed that blood and water with which we have been renewed. And that's our way of saying, *"It's all right."*

And finally, we're at this Mass where bread shall be taken, and wine brought up and changed into the body and blood of Christ, and broken and crushed and given, because today Jesus is still saying, "This is my body given for you. This is my blood shed for you and for the one who has died." And this, above all, is our greatest assurance that God pats us on the head and says, *"It's all right."*

So we go back to the altar with that double stream of feeling: human grief and loss, especially having known someone who suffered a long time. A sense of relief that it's all over because it's been a long, hard road for everybody. A sense of bewilderment, facing death so squarely and closely. But above all, I hope, a sense of faith. Faith that God gives us in our collective selves and this ancient liturgy. And faith in the promises that God made, the pat on the head, the allaying of our fears, the uplifting of our hopes, the forgiveness of our anger, the strengthening of our faith, and the promise that through Jesus, as our liturgy says, life is never ended but merely exchanged. And so for N., as for us, "It's all right."

Sue, a Name on the Wall

(JOHN 15:12–17)

The deceased is a middle-aged woman who worked for Meridian Health Services, heroically battling cancer before succumbing. She was a wonderful amateur artist whom I met in art class and then recognized as a parishioner. The chief imagery here is the Vietnam Wall.

A few years ago, I had the opportunity to make a trip to Washington, DC, with some friends. Part of our itinerary was a visit to the Vietnam Memorial Wall. As you may know, the monument is a long black granite wall with thousands of names of those who lost their lives in the war. As I walked the grounds of the memorial, a couple of things stood out. The first thing I noticed was the silence. As crowded as it was, there was a hush of reverence over the whole setting. The next thing that caught my eye was how different people approached the wall, once they found the name of a loved one. They moved very slowly as if approaching something sacred and would then touch the name. Some stood quietly, running their fingers gently over the letters. Others wept, and some even knelt.

As I watched this ritual unfold before my eyes, I couldn't help but wonder what the relationship was between the living person and the name. It had to be something special or it would not have solicited such a reaction. After all, there were literally hundreds of people milling about the wall and some were obviously just there as spectators. They could touch lots of names on the wall and have no reaction whatsoever. To them, the names were just letters carved in a wall. But to others, those names, or rather, *this* name, was a cause for tears.

When I go to cemeteries at someone's funeral I have noticed a similar response when people come to pay their respects to a loved one. Out of the corner of my eye I see them walk past rows and rows of names on monuments and crypts looking for just one. Then they stop. They approach a special stone with reverence and run their fingers over the carved letters that spell out the name of their loved ones. Some weep, others are just still, lost in grief or reverie.

So where is the connection? As I said, it is in the relationship. To those who knew the person behind the name, it represents all the memories, the history, the personality and intimacy created between these two people. It is the depth of the relationship that makes the connection. It isn't just in the name. It represents the investment of life one person made in another person. It represents someone who made a difference to somebody.

That's the way it is here this morning. To many, to most perhaps in Point Pleasant, Sue Van Benthuysen is but a name on the wall, a name in the obituary column of the *Press*, some person who died much too young at age fifty-four. But for us, it's different. There are enough of us here in this church today who do have cause to remember Sue, who run our fingers over her name and pause, and weep and pray and smile and remember.

As we touch those letters, we conjure up memories of this little girl who at the tender age of five moved with her family from Newark to Point Pleasant. Some remember her graduation from Georgian Court, the birth of her son, the loss of her father seven years ago, the devotion of her mother and siblings, the delight of her nieces and nephews. We know also that, beyond her immediate family, there are many acquaintances, for Sue was, like a child gathering snowflakes, a natural gatherer of friends. She worked for the Meridian Health Systems for many years and had many friends there, some of whom are here today. She had special friends, among whom Rosemary Doherty stands out. My own memories of friendship as I run my fingers over her name are that of a gracious, generous, and talented lady whom I met, of all places, at art class. I had almost no talent. Sue had a great deal of it. I used to silently watch with envy her painting come to life as mine languished in dullsville. Soon we became acquainted and I felt more comfortable watching her, openly hoping to get some hints. She was a wonderful painter.

Then almost accidentally we began to meet here at St. Martha's and she suddenly realized that the bumbling pupil was a priest and I suddenly realized that she was a gentle person of gentle faith, a wonderful woman. As time went on, she told me of her cancer, her battle, her remission, and then, lately, its return; as it turned out, its final return. We met. We talked about it. We prayed. She knew time was short and tried to prepare herself. I hadn't seen her at church for a while, figuring that we missed each other, until her mother called last Friday to say that Sue was dying and I went over to the house and gave her the sacrament of the sick and dying. She, my good friend, died the next day.

And as I say this, I remember: there's that word again, the one that appeared in our gospel: "I have called you friends....you did not choose me but I chose you and I appointed you to go and bear fruit, fruit that will last." This woman, Sue, had the greatest Friend of all. She *was* chosen, chosen at her baptism and she has remained true to her call and God has remained true to her. That white cloth over her coffin is but her original baptismal dress stretched large to remind us that she ends up where he began: in God's house, as God's child, as God's friend. The white vestments of joy that I am wearing are a symbol of the happiness of that enduring friendship, a reminder that the fruit of her life lives on in so many here. The flowers you see here are a sign that her life has bloomed. The light of the Easter Candle here is a sign of new life and, at the same time, a guarantee what she is now with the One who chose her, bright with love.

As the poet says:

Is there a leaf upon the tree
The Father does not see?
Leaves fall, so do we all
Return to earth, to sod.
Sparrows and kings,
And all manner of things
Fall, fall into the hands
Of the living God

Sue has fallen. She has been caught.
May she rest in peace in those Loving Arms. Amen.

Mike, in Need of a Story

(JOHN 14:1–3)

The focus for the homilist here is the wonderful story by Arthur Gordon and its connection to the gospel. It's a great and comforting story and can be used in many configurations for a funeral.

I noticed in his official obituary that Michael Capenegro, *Colonel* Michael Capenegro, had a distinguished career. He was an infantry officer for twenty-five years and he was a professor of Military Science and, after military retirement, he taught at St. John's School of Business, not to mention that he was also mayor of this township for more than ten years. Impressive. I strain to picture this talented man in these challenging roles, imagining him both in and out of uniform as straightforward, competent, undertaking his various duties with confidence, and doing his tasks with level-headed integrity. I am indeed taken with his bio and am in awe of his achievements and appreciate them dearly. His was an admirable and useful life.

But I have to confess that this marvelous resume I try so hard to keep in mind keeps dissolving into the wellsprings of my emotions, perhaps because I did not know him as a colonel or professor or politician. The fact is, whatever his achievements, I knew him simply as a man and I loved not the colonel or the professor or the politician, but Mike. Just as, I know, his family knew and loved him as husband,

father, brother, cousin, grandfather. These levels, these heart connections, these poignant memories—each one cherished to the point of
tears, each one turned over, examined, held tightly and traded these
past few days—no obituary can capture.

As for me, we met casually and respectfully in his post-military
days when I first came to St. Mary's. But over the years we drew closer as I sensed something special and honorable about him. When his
lovely wife, Ramona, died, I presided at her Mass as I am, sadly, doing
at his; and I got to know him better, bound by a common event.

Then, in the course of time a widow from Middletown, Peg Boyle,
caught his eye. This was another link because I knew Peg and her
husband and family previously when, as a young priest—alas, a long
time ago—I was stationed in St. Mary's in Middletown. A good woman from my past and a good man from my present built a new life, a
good life, as they should have, and I was a part of it. But I think the
bond was cemented because of two things. First, Mike was a faith-
filled man. I admired that. He was true to his religion, loyal to his
parish, and regular in his worship, and that's no small thing, no small
witness. Second, most of all, as far as I was selfishly concerned, he
liked me. He was very supportive. He backed up my efforts, praised
my homilies, volunteered, like so many, for parish projects. He, like
Peg, was simply there, and being there, like Woody Allen's showing
up, is the stuff of life and a badge of honor.

But I tell you, what remains in my memory is after I left St. Mary's.
On occasions, usually funerals, unfortunately, I would come back.
Mike, who always attended daily Mass, would always intercept me
afterward. And the routine was always the same: I can picture it now.
Silently, in the back of church, with that manly grin on his face, he
would stand directly in front of me, extend his right hand to my right
hand to hold, take his left hand and place it on my shoulder and look
me straight in the eye and say sincerely, "How are you? It's good to
see you." He meant every word.

I mention this because he in fact, like some others have done, said
to me after one of those funerals, "Father, I liked that story. When I
die I want you to come back and tell it to my family." I replied casu-

ally, "OK, Mike, it's a deal. And if I go before you, I hereby give you permission to read it at *my* funeral." And we both laughed. And afterward, whenever I came back for a funeral, he would point his finger at me and say, "Remember!" and I would give him a thumbs up.

And here I am, unexpectedly, with heavy heart, redeeming my promise.

Ironically, as some of you here will recall, the story he wanted is one I gave here precisely a week ago in this same church in connection with a lenten series I was giving. The story is a variation on the gospel I read. You recall, Jesus, likely with his own next-day death in mind, knowing what abandonment and fear were like as he would experience them in the garden of Gethsemane, wanted to give some comfort to his soon-to-be bereaved disciples. So, as you heard, he said, "Do not let your hearts be troubled...in my Father's house there are many dwelling places....I go to prepare a place for you....I will come again and take you to myself so that where I am you may be also...."

So here, for Mike and his family, is that gospel dressed up in the story he wanted.

A long time ago there lived a little boy whose parents had died. He was taken in by an aunt who raised him as her own child. Years later, after he had grown up and left his aunt, he received a letter from her. She was in terminal illness and, from the tone of her letter, he knew she was afraid of death. This man, whom she had raised and touched, wrote her a letter in which he said:

It is now thirty-five years since I, a little boy of six, was left quite alone in the world. You sent me word that you would give me a home and be a mother to me. I've never forgotten the day when I made the long journey of ten miles to your house. I can still recall my disappointment when, instead of coming for me yourself, you sent your servant, Caesar, a dark man, to fetch me. I well remember my tears and my anxiety as, perched high on your horse and clinging tight to Caesar, I rode off to my new home.

Night fell before we finished the journey and as it grew dark, I became even more afraid. "Do you think she'll go to bed before I get there?" I asked Caesar anxiously.

"Oh, no," said Caesar, "she's sure to stay up for you. When we get out of these woods, you'll see her light shining in the window."

Presently, we did ride out into the clearing and there was your light. I remember that you were waiting at the door, that you put your arms tight around me, that you lifted me, a tired, frightened little boy, down from the horse. You had a fire burning on the hearth, a hot supper waiting on the stove. After supper you took me to my new room. You heard me say my prayers. Then you sat with me until I fell asleep.

You probably realize why I am trying to recall this to your memory now. Very soon, God is going to send for you, and take you to a new home. I'm trying to tell you that you needn't be afraid of the summons or of the strange journey or of the dark messenger of death. God can be trusted. God can be trusted to do as much for you as you did for me so many years ago.

At the end of the road you'll find love and a welcome waiting. And you'll be safe in God's care. I'm going to watch and pray for you until you're out of sight. And I shall wait for the day when I make the same journey myself and find you waiting at the end of the road to greet me.

Notice the metaphors and symbols: Caesar, the dark figure, is death; the light at the end of he journey is Jesus, the light of the world. The house is the "many rooms" in the Father's house that Jesus promised. The supper is the heavenly banquet. God is the loving aunt. It's a homecoming story. It is gospel.

Well, I hope you are pleased, Mike, not only that I kept my promise, but that you have found the story to be true and have arrived at your Father's house safely. And as for you, Peg—and also for you, Frances, Michael, Lorri, and John; and Josephine, Grace, Rocco, Alfred, and Sonny and the in-laws and grandchildren—I hope the comfort this thoughtful man wanted me to convey to you has found its mark in your hearts.

What more can I say? Be sad that he's gone. Be glad that he's home.

Ralph, Deep Down

(JOHN 20:19–21)

I've included the gospel here to show that I shortened it for my purposes. This homily was very well received and, to my surprise, it struck a note with some in the congregation whose parents had fallen into dementia or Alzheimer's disease. The homily was, I found, an enormous comfort to survivors to know that God reached "deep down" into the mental sickness and dimness to bring peace to their loved ones. Recommended for people who did have mind-destroying diseases.

On the evening of that first day of the week, when the doors were closed where the disciples were, for fear of the authorities, Jesus came and stood in their midst and said to them, "Peace be with you." When he said this, he showed them his hands and his side. The disciples rejoiced when they saw the Lord. Jesus said to them again, "Peace be with you. As the Father has sent me, so I send you." And when he had said this he breathed on them and said to them, "Receive the Holy Spirit...."

The Gospel of the Lord.

There is, I suppose, some significance that Ralph Imholte—husband, father, grandfather, deacon, friend—died just as the Easter season was beginning, Holy Saturday morning to be exact, because he was, as you

know, very much an Easter person. He was springtime with his boom-
ing voice, his athletic prowess, his contagious hugs, which he scattered
like Johnny Appleseed. He was sometimes stubborn, quite sentimen-
tal, always sensitive. He was a passionate man, passionate with people,
passionate with God. I knew that right off when I first met him.

You recall, as I mentioned at the funeral of Rosemary, his childhood sweetheart, his lifelong love, that I first encountered Ralph
when, a transplant from Minnesota and a fugitive from St. Leo's at
that time, he snuck over here to St. Mary's, and eventually, like Caesar, he came, he saw, he liked, and he conquered.

He asked outright if I would sponsor him as a deacon and I agreed
on the condition that he find and dedicate himself to a particular
ministry. In tribute to his wife, he said proudly that he was happily
married and would like to share that. So the parish sent him to Iona
College and then to Seton Hall to get his degree in counseling and in
1977 he was ordained a deacon.

To make a long, familiar story short, he became so good that we
hired him to do all our marriage preparation and counseling, and
what an asset over the years he was to the parish! Then, to keep him
around all the time, I made him Parish Administrator. A good deal,
I thought: deacon, counselor, parish administrator, and eventually
friend, all in one package! How lucky could we get? He had settled in
to St. Mary's and we were never the same.

Ralph, as you know, was a force, a glue. With his six-foot physique
and bald head, looking for all the world like an understudy for Mr.
Clean, later to be graced by a beard, he was hard not to notice. His
buoyant presence was always signaled by a hearty laugh, a shouted
exclamation, unbounded energy. He was part of a loyal faith-sharing
group, went off annually to Weston Priory with his friends, gave
Pre-Cana conferences and various courses. Many a happy marriage
today owes itself to his ministrations. He was a trusted collaborator,
a co-laborer, very much an essential part of the color and charism
of St. Mary's.

It was, therefore, for all of us, a shock when this jock, this jogger,
this competitive player who gave his sons a run for their money on

the handball and tennis courts, had a stroke. Well, the long and short of it was that, despite our hopes, he never recovered. Rosemary put her ills on the back burner and ministered to him and, when she died, he died inside. We could all see that.

The seamless trip from hospital to rehab to nursing home was as inevitable as it was sad. To see this once big, vital man reduced to helplessness, this marathon man confined to a wheelchair, was hard to take. His loving and faithful family and his loyal friends could sense the slow decline. When I saw him last, it was clear that he had almost completely collapsed into his inner core, that he no longer could focus or recognize outside.

Yet speaking of that, there is, I suggest, some significance that Ralph did die on Holy Saturday. Let me digress as I tell you why. When I was a little boy the old pious folk used to call Holy Saturday "Deep-Down Day," an odd term. I used to wonder what it meant, so one day I asked my uncle. In his funny accent he said to me, "Little One"—he always called me "Little One—it means that Jesus, you know, went deep, deep down, went down there." He pointed to the ground. Seeing my blank face, he went on. "Jesus, you know, after he died, went to the deep hell."

Immediately I recognized that phase from the creed, "He descended into hell," and I remember Sister telling us in school that it meant that, after he died, Jesus went to the underworld to rescue all those waiting in a kind of antechamber to lead them triumphantly to a heretofore closed paradise. When I repeated that to my uncle, trying to enlighten him, he shook his head and, being a better theologian than Sister was, said patiently, "No, Little One, it means that there is no place Jesus cannot be." And much, much later I understood what he was saying.

I came to understand that Jesus, going deep down, descending into hell, means that when we are paralyzed by fear or sickness, locked behind the closed doors of our broken bodies and dimmed minds, God can still come, stand inside our fears and paralysis, and breathe out peace. "He descended into hell" means there is no hell where Jesus cannot, will not, be. As we heard in the gospel, they haven't built a door yet that his love cannot pass through.

So when Ralph died on "Deep-Down Saturday" I knew right away that this is what happened to him. In the last months and weeks of his life, our beloved friend had slowly faded behind closed doors—his diminishing body, his vacant eyes—and we were no longer able to enter. But Deep-Down Saturday tells me that there was one who *could* enter, who *did* enter, to stand in the middle of his fear, his darkness, to give him comfort, and to breathe peace into the depths of his soul.

Jesus went through Ralph's closed doors to be with him, exhale the Spirit, and lead him home. I knew then that Saturday's deep-down love had brought Sunday's resurrection to my friend and I cried and smiled at the same time.

Whitey, Kathy, Mary Jo, Tom, Mark, and all Ralph's family and friends, hold that image in mind: the Easter Triduum—Good Friday, Deep-Down Saturday, and Risen Sunday—will always be linked to father, deacon, friend Ralph Imholte and each anniversary will give us sufficient reason through our tears to sing the Easter Alleluia.

Amen.

As I end and depart this pulpit, I must admit that there are two things that tease my mind: First, what must be his meeting with Rosemary? Second, was even Jesus prepared for his bear hug?

Easter peace, dear friend.

Mary, Wife and Weaver

The deceased was a lovely, quiet woman of the parish. The imagery here is that of a weaver, one who quietly weaves together the fabric of a holy life. She had buried a son, Peter, a year or so before.

I first met Mary, or rather, perhaps, I was first more aware of her when, at church a long time ago, I was trying to build a sense of community. She always sat around the fourth or fifth pew to my right in those days. It was the feast of Epiphany, the feast of strangers from a strange place coming to Christ, and I said that Epiphany *still* takes place and we're all proofs of that. Then I proceeded to say that my father was of German descent, an orphan early on who wound up in Hightstown and he met my mother, an immigrant from Italy. And here I am in Colts Neck. And then I went around and invited other people to reveal their distant origins.

And people, some of you might recall, stood up and called out their country of ancestry: Ireland, Spain, Italy, France, Chile, Belgium, and so on. I said, "See, we're from all over, but united here in the same search and faith, just like the Wise Men. I guess we've covered all the countries." Then a timid woman raised her hand. I looked at her and asked, "Did we forget someone?" She smiled, gave that little-girl shrug, and said, "American Indian." I shot back, "Foreigner!" It was, of course, Mary Vanderbilt slyly letting me know that I had overlooked the obvious. I made a mental note to keep an eye on that woman.

I did, and over time I found out that she was a rather remarkable woman and that her frail frame belied someone who had a long and hard journey from harsh poverty to tragic widowhood, to marriage to a man who would worship her all her life, and to motherhood that produced a large family she would nurture in good times and in bad. In fact, Mary reminded me of a TV interview I once saw.

The person being interviewed happened to be a heroic mother who had single-handedly raised a large family. In spite of all the frustrations, disappointments, and obstacles, she had persevered, and every one of her children had remarkable achievements not only in their schooling, but also in their vocation. It was an inspiring story worth celebrating, for it revealed the heights and depths of human greatness. During the interview, the reporter asked the mother her secret: 'I suppose you loved all your children equally, making sure that all got the same treatment?" The mother replied, "I loved them. I loved them all, each one of them, but not equally. I loved the one the most who was down until he was up. I loved the one the most who was weak until she was strong. I loved the one the most who was hurt until he was healed. I loved the one the most who was lost until she was found." That was Mary Vanderbilt.

That love wasn't confined to her husband and children either. In my book, she took a giant step up when I learned that she was wild about dogs and she would often bring Lady, who always remained ladylike, even when my dog barked at her to let her know she was on his property. And, I discovered, she had a deft way with antiques and would come over to the annual Chinese auction and appraise the hidden treasures among the junk.

But mostly I learned what great faith she and Doug had when together they ministered to their son Peter, embraced his illness, and eventually buried him, not, however, before Peter, true son of his mother and father, volunteered to refinish for me the wood altar in the spiritual center chapel. And then she would ferry the leftover food from Delicious Orchards to the place in Neptune that had been so supportive of Peter. Faith, hope, and love seemed to ride easy with her.

I want to confess something. I have this automatic mental habit of labeling people, a kind of seeing people in symbolic occupations and so, quite unconsciously, somewhere along the way—I don't remember when—I got this mental image of Mary Vanderbilt as a *weaver*. Yes, that was it. Perfect. Like an invisible thread, she quietly wove together a family and this community. She was always a background person helping out here and there, stuffing bulletins, cleaning up, making life easier. Yes, no doubt, she was a weaver of lives, of faith, of joy.

I was stunned when I heard she was in the hospital. That, to no one's surprise, her husband and her children rallied around her so attentively, took tender care of her to the end, and were generous in their love says a great deal about the way she raised them. And still, you know what? Even in the hospital, when she rallied slightly, she sent me this birthday card—What a woman!—I have here. The front, showing berries and butterflies, reads, "How blessed we are with little gifts from God." And then, inside, in her handwriting, these words, "Dear Father, We shall be forever grateful for all that you have brought to our lives. Our appreciation for you and our affection for you run so very, very deep. Our warmest love, Mary and Doug."

Here she is, with a few days left in her life, taking time to express love. How like her, how *very* like her, this weaver to the last. I shall always cherish this card and save it not only for its message, but because those words on the front say everything I could possibly say about Mary Vanderbilt, "How blessed we are with little gifts from God."

Amen to that.

$\mathcal{Doug}$, the Waiter

To no one's surprise Mary's husband died about two years later. They were in love and he could not endure the separation. The imagery here, as one might expect, is that of a waiter.

There are all kinds of waiters. I don't mean the folk who wait on your table at restaurants, but people who wait. Period. They fall into several distinctive categories and styles.

There are those who remain patient and calm no matter what the circumstance, but they are rare. Far more common are the impatient who pace and foot-tap and steal glances at their watches; who, when you finally arrive, let you know exactly how late you are; who maddeningly weave in and out of parkway traffic, trying to get one car ahead of the others; who jockey to get into the express lane at the supermarket with their far over-twelve limit; who, like the White Rabbit, are always in a hurry.

Then there are the waiters who bring something to read. Next there are the multi-taskers with their ubiquitous cell phones and Palm Pilots who, conditioned by society's incessant noise, can't abide the solitude and silence so necessary for emotional and spiritual growth. There are those who practice a Zen-like calm, whose motto is, "When they arrive, they arrive." Their opposite is the overanxious, who spend their time letting their imagination run wild, sure that something terrible and disastrous has happened, like the kidnapping of their awaited friend or their falling through an open manhole or being abducted by aliens. There are those who simply can't wait at all, like the child asking "Are we there yet?" or "When is Santa coming?" Finally, there are those for whom waiting is sublime, like a woman awaiting the birth of a child who is taken in by the experience, or like a husband awaiting reunion with his wife.

That's how I think of this gentle man, Doug Vanderbilt. Waiter. Doug was never the same after Mary died. He became essentially a year-and-a half-long Advent person, yearning for the wife of many years and the God who would make them one again. Perhaps, therefore, it is fitting that he would go to his spouse and to the Lord during the season of expectation, the time of holy longing. His wait is over.

You know, I can still picture him at Mary's funeral in March of last year, how he perked up and looked at me when I read a note they had both sent me, a note made even more precious because Mary was at that time in the hospital and Doug was faithfully at her side, morning, noon, and night. Yet they took time to send a card that I still have and cherish. How I remember its words: "Dear Father, we shall be forever grateful for all that you have brought into our lives. Our appreciation for you and our affection for you run so very, very deep. Our warmest love. Mary and Doug." I brought to *their* lives? That still embarrasses me. What about all they brought to the lives of their children, to the lives of their friends, to the lives of this community, to my life and yours?

In Mary's homily, some may remember, I called her a weaver, a thread that wove together family, friends, and community. Now I call Doug a waiter, an Advent waiter who, according to Kip, when the doctor told him that he had a few weeks to live, protested that it was too long. He was leaving sooner. You cannot frustrate love.

I was privileged to anoint Doug last Sunday, to bring him the presence and comfort of the church, the fruits of Jesus' death and resurrection. He was quite conscious of my being there—our being there—and rewarded me with a smile of recognition. With the anointing done, I knew it was the last thing to be tucked away and he was ready and willing to depart. He had a reunion to attend.

Weaver and waiter, joined by the power of that Child we all yearn for at this holy season, the Child who one day would declare, "Come to me, all of you who labor and are burdened and I will give you rest." And whose resurrection would be a promise of our own.

Advent expectation has been met even before the season is over. May he rest in the faith that he practiced. May he rest in the hope that he kept. May he rest in the lady-love that he cherished. May this good man, this husband, father, grandfather, this friend, rest in peace. Amen.

Helen, on the Road to Emmaus

(LUKE 24:13–35)

Helen was part of the "Morning Group," those people who came to daily Mass and who so generously took on many domestic and parochial tasks, such as stuffing the bulletin every Friday. We always had a pot of coffee going and people took turns bringing goodies. The imagery here is drawn from the powerful Emmaus story, and I have used its divisions as points of commentary.

When St. Luke sat down to write this gospel story, it was not just a fancy and interesting telling of a post-resurrection tale. He was writing for his community that, like so many other communities—like our own today—had to face the question of death. And with death, the feeling of isolation, loss, shattering distress, and, often, as in the case of Helen, relief, for it was a hard departure. And in his finely wrought story Luke has proposed three elements as to how a community, a family, can find its own inner healing when faced with death, as the apostles did when faced with the death of its leader, Jesus Christ.

Notice the first element in Luke's story: the Scriptures. When these bewildered and distressed and grieving disciples were excitedly talking on the way to Emmaus, the stranger approached, and after their exchange of news, what did he do after he listened to their distress, anxiety, and hurt? *He opened to them the Scriptures.* And thus Luke is saying, in effect, in *your* grief, in *your* facing death—the death of your mother, your sister, your aunt, your grandmom—the first step to healing is to open up the Scriptures. And so we open them and as we cast our eye here and there, what is it we read? We read of Jesus saying: "I am the resurrection and the life; he who believes in me shall never die." Helen believed in Jesus. Or again, "The one who would save his life will lose it, but the one who loses his life for my sake shall find it." Helen, in her gifts to her family and to her church, often "lost" her life. And again in the Scriptures through Isaiah: "Though your sins be as red as scarlet I will make them as white as snow." Or yet, in Jeremiah, "Behold, tell the people I have loved you with an everlasting love." Helen was much loved, by God and by us.

And so Luke is right: The Scriptures give us comfort, and that is why through those words we can celebrate this woman's death in hope, because Jesus is now her resurrection and new life. And because of this we take our very human tears and our deep sorrow and freely mingle them with hope and, in a certain sense, even with joy. Which is why, from the very beginning, Christians have always displayed that double feeling about death: the profound sorrow at losing someone they have known and loved, right along with a very distinct undercurrent of joy. And the church, you observe, picks that up in its liturgy. For example, we have flowers that we normally associate with joyous times. And we are wearing the white vestments that we associate with weddings. And, what's more, in the early church, if they had had newspapers, the headline for Helen would even have been: "Helen Owendoff Celebrates Her Birthday Today." Because in the old days, they considered the day you died your birth-day, when you were really born again, when, without encumbrance and without obliqueness, without hospitals and medications, without pain and machines, without tubes and coma, directly face to face, as Paul says, you would look on the vision and the face of the Father. And all this because the Scriptures opened up to us the meaning of life and death in Jesus.

The second element that Luke gives for healing is the teaching that the distraught and grieving disciples finally recognized Jesus in the breaking of the bread. That is, in the Eucharist we get a glimpse—we always do—that we are not alone either in life or death, but that we recognize, however dimly, that One is at table with us, abides with us: "I am the bread of life. The one who eats this bread and drinks this blood abides in me and I will raise him up on the last day." Helen, who so often broke bread here around this very altar and therefore had intimations that she was never alone, now knows for sure. The Christ who came to her in the shadow of bread and wine is now there in the brightness of full humanity and friendship. She sees clearly now what she only surmised when she worshipped with us. And it is glorious.

The final element that Luke gives us in coming to terms with death is community. You notice at the end of his story, the first thing the disciples did when they got the good news of the Scriptures and recognized Jesus in the breaking of the bread, they turned around and went back to the community at Jerusalem. And here's the final element in the healing of the grieving heart, immersion in the community: the community of one's family and friends, the community of the church, the community we call parish. It is in this faith community that we freely exchange our hurts, our pains, our hopes, our love, and, in the context of such faith, healing eventually takes place.

But Helen knew all about that because she was certainly a force in this community. Oh, without any effort I can easily see her now all over the place: the counter of money, the reader of the Scriptures, the stuffer of bulletins, the Martha/Mary member, the chatty reporter of news far and wide, the bright and witty energy of the morning group. And I can see her too as the pray-er in the pews, the mother who twenty-three years ago buried a son in this very church, the wife who mourned a husband four years ago, the pilgrim whom God wondrously led from Brooklyn to Morris Plains to ultimately grace us at St. Mary's and then who journeyed from Lincroft to Monroe Township, the remarkably young looking and agile senior citizen who was an inspiration to us all. She was no doubt a vital strand in the fabric of community.

The Scriptures, Eucharist, Community: Luke's formula still works. And so, having tested it once more, we now we say goodbye to this woman of fourscore and six years. She mattered to her family and friends. She mattered to us. She made a difference, and that is high praise. She made us laugh, which is even higher. She cherished the Scriptures, ate at the table of the Lord, and enlarged community, which is the highest praise. She is now the journey completed. May she rest in peace.

Bill, Another Ananias

(LUKE 12:32–34)

This homily also taps into the "behind the scene" theme, this time using the comparison to the scriptural Ananias. The first reading was a condensed form of his story from the Acts of the Apostles.

I have but a few, brief, very simple words as befits a man who would cringe at any long, flowery oration, so here they are. As many of you know, the Christian world is celebrating the afterglow of Easter. In this period our daily Scripture readings are taken from Luke's idealized early church history, the Acts of the Apostles.

In the first part of his work, he focuses on Peter and in the second part, just begun, he focuses on Paul. He starts with Paul's conversion. He relates how Paul, an enemy of his fellow Jews who claimed Jesus as Messiah, went around harassing and arresting them. But on the way to Damascus to claim more victims, he has a vision of Jesus, is struck blind, and told to wait for further instructions.

Meanwhile, in a little side street, a little unknown shoemaker, obviously a recent convert to the Way, as the Jesus Movement was called, has a vision. His name in Ananias. He's told to go to a street named Straight—easy to find in a city notorious for its wickedly crooked alleys—to find Paul and cure him. Ananias protests, citing Paul's murderous reputation toward his kind. He's overruled, gets himself moving, and with great trepidation finds Paul, cures his blindness (physical and spiritual), and baptizes him. Paul, as we know, eventually goes on to fame, if not fortune, on Oprah and the cover of *Time*.

And Ananias? The truth is, he goes on to nothing. His task done, he simply goes back to his shoe shop, lives, works, and dies. Period. This man, a non-entity, comes and goes and is never heard of again. There is, as far as I know, no *Saint* Ananias. No church named after him, no statue, no feast day. And yet—yet—we have to stop and ponder this deep truth about this little man of Scripture: He was there when God needed him and, in the end, that was all that mattered.

When you come to think of it, the Bible, life itself, is full of such "Ananias" people who are simply "there" when needed, with a capital "T."

You can see where I'm heading. I'm heading to Bill Kozabo, who, along with Helen, was a true Ananias, the best praise I can bestow. This quiet man of St. Joseph's trade was there when his country needed him: He was a sailor in the war. He was there when his community needed him: years as a fire and first aid volunteer. And finally and gratefully, to come to my personal experience, he was there when St Mary's needed him, when I needed him.

When I first met Bill and Helen some thirty-five years ago—is it that long?—I knew I had met my Ananias. From the beginning, they were emotionally and spiritually with me and were delighted with the new life beginning at St. Mary's. They readily embraced all the activities, the "coming alive" as Helen said more than once. There they were when we navigated Manhattan on the Circle Line. They were there in one of the dozen buses taking us to the old Madison Square Garden or Radio City. They were there at every event. Good and prayerful people, they were there every Sunday, They were there in the parish ministries and in every phase of St. Mary's journey to this very day.

What I'm trying to say, perhaps not too well, is that their "thereness," the simple, loyal, precious fact of it, was such a support and comfort and a grace, an outward sign of God's fidelity. As a result, over the years, like so many of you, we grew beyond parish priest and parishioner into friends. And then, I recall, in those days when Margaret was sick, I went many times to the Kozabo house to care for her and wound up being cared for. I never left the house without a treat.

And what do you say about people who for thirty-five years, uninterruptedly, have sent me a card, not only every Christmas, but on every single anniversary and every birthday?

We have had, thank God, our St. Pauls from this parish, names known and celebrated. But we have also had, and do have, thank God, our Ananiases, the "there" people, and this quiet man of integrity and faith, Bill Kozabo, was near the top of the list. People like him are simply glue, fabric weavers, mosaics in the grand design of love, life, and God's kingdom and that's all that matters.

I liked Bill, loved him and Helen and Margaret Buckelew. I was sorry to hear about his illness. When I did, I visited him in the Care One Home. He was alert, kidded about Helen's visit at the hairdressers when I asked about her. It was a nice visit, alas, my last one. Then apparently things grew worse and the last months were painful and excruciating for everyone and I'm sure that Helen and family and friends have to be relieved that at last Bill is relieved.

And now we come to pray for and bury this man thus relieved, noting that as St. Luke had his Acts of the Apostles and his Ananias, St. Mary's has its memories and its Bill Kozabos.

It is a sad time for all of us, but the happy note as I end my simple words for a simple man is this: The one thing I am absolutely sure of is that when God needed Bill, Bill was there for God. And now that Bill needs God, God is there for him. You can count on it.

Husband, uncle, carpenter, sailor, volunteer, parishioner, friend—good and faithful servant, may you rest in peace. Amen.

Hans, the Blessed

In this homily I explore the theme of Advent for a gentle man waiting to die.

The gospel I just read is from the first Sunday of Advent and it ended, as you heard, with the words, "What I say to you, I say to all: 'Watch.'" Hans Ziegler was an Advent man, a watchful man. Not a fatalist who embraced cynicism but a realist who embraced acceptance.

He was eighty-nine years old. His health was failing. He was four years in a convalescent home, and he knew he would never leave. But as he wrote so typically in his Christmas note this year, "This is the fourth Christmas I am spending in a nursing home, and thanks to the continued care, and especially the loving help from my dear family and loyal friends, I have been fortunate to adjust to this limited lifestyle as an acceptable old-age solution. The fourth year passed without any major medical crisis and to expect at age eighty-nine further significant health improvements would seem to be unrealistic. (A lovely understatement.) It is time to count one's blessings!"

That's Hans Ziegler. That's a man at peace with himself. I always found him with that peace, for he used his time to pray and to count those blessings. Among his blessings he counted, above all, his family. He missed his beloved wife, Frederica, but he was mightily interested in the children and their children. Many times when I went to visit him, he would give me chapter and verse about each member: their travel, address changes, love lives. He delighted to see them unfold into mature adults. He was very proud of you.

He counted his friends a blessing too. The staff at the home, the visitors, Sister Agnes, and others. He also counted as a blessing and felt vindicated and proud when a book came out this year entitled *From Space to Earth*, in which the author mentioned him by name and his activities, some forty years ago, in the Signal Corps' Space Program. He was quite pleased with that.

Most of all, I know, he counted his faith a blessing. He spent his forced contemplative time in bed in prayer, in thought, in preparation, and in deepening that faith. Knowing that the time was coming near, but not when, he stayed alert as a faithful disciple. To me, he was a kind of living Advent: waiting and watching. Coincidentally, I saw him four days before he died. Sister Agnes had called to tell me he was taken to Jersey Shore Hospital. She thought I'd like to know, although she kidded that the last time she called me and I rushed over he returned from the hospital better than before! Still, I didn't want to take chances and I left immediately. When I got to the emergency ward he was not there. He was having x-rays taken. I ran into an old St. Mary's parishioner who was a nurse there and a parishioner from St. Denis where I helped out. We chatted as I waited and they brought Hans back. As they rolled him around into the cubicle where he could see me—I can still see his expression—he was delighted. Tired but still sharp—his mind was always clear—he spoke to me. He said it was hard, all these ups and downs, but what can you do?

He talked about his family as always, accepted with great joy and faith the blessing I gave and thanked me dearly for coming. He profoundly embarrassed me—I was glad no one was around to overhear him—when he said it was like a visit from Jesus Christ. Whatever his impression, I left an eighty-nine-year-old man who sensed he was dying at peace. And as I left, I must say, under my breath, I thanked him for his friendship and example and inspiration and wondered who was the real Christ.

I don't want to canonize the man. I've only known him for about twenty-some years. I don't know his early life and whether he was mean at times or had a temper or what weaknesses he had. I only know what I saw from the time I met him: a man with a keen mind who in years developed a deep faith and in his illness a profound belief that, in the end, love would be stronger than death. And so it has been.

The Lord of the house has come suddenly during Advent and found Hans not sleeping, but watching, and because he did heed the Lord's words of warning to watch, I am sure he has also heard the Lord's words of promise for those who do: "Well done, good and faithful servant. Enter into the joy of the Lord." Amen.

Bob, Classmate and Priest

Bob, a classmate for part of my seminary days, went to a different seminary for his theology. We knew each other but were not close. That's why I was surprised when he had left instructions that I should preach, not at this funeral Mass but at the special memorial Mass that is customary the day or so before the main funeral. I exploit my lack of common friendship to explore the larger bonds that unite priests.

It is only right that I should be forthright with you. When Father Jawidzik called me the other night not only to tell me that Father Heller had died—he had been ill for about ten years, I understand—but that he had left it in his will that I should give the homily at this commemoration Mass, I was dumbfounded. Was this some kind of a mischievous, impish thing he would do on occasion? What did the man have in mind? Was he of sound mind when he put that in his will?

You see, the truth of the matter is that, beyond the accident of us being classmates and being ordained together forty years ago on June 4, 1955, as the last class to be ordained there before the old cathedral burned down—some, I confess, saw that as a judgment—we never had much contact. Hardly any. We went our separate ways. We did not go out socially, did not meet, and I think the last time I saw him was some twenty years ago when he was pastor at St. Ambrose in Browntown and I spoke at Father Ed Griswold's first Mass there. Father Griswold was the alternative preacher for this homily in case I couldn't make it, but he is away, I understand, and so I am here. But why, I am not sure. Bob and I were not close.

Which means, as I hinted, because of my social and physical distance from Father Heller, that I am here as one not only perplexed as to why he choose me, but as one also really unable to speak of personal things or give a eulogy. Fortunately, tomorrow at his funeral Mass, Father Bill Haughney, who knew him better, will do such homiletic honors.

So I stand here before you and my deceased classmate, slightly embarrassed and quite humbled, with nothing in common to talk about, which spares you many words, and maybe, when you come down to it, that might be his last and cunning gift to you.

Nothing in common...except, perhaps, when I think about it, two things that we *do* share: our human journey and our priesthood.

For our human journeys necessarily coincide: from childhood to youth to adulthood and mature years with all of their successes and failures, health and sickness, sins and repentances. To that degree I recognize that body before us and know its spirit: It is you and me. A lifetime is squeezed into that little box, but it is, of course, a lifetime larger than that container, for it's a lifetime that has changed lives, forged friendships, made its mark, and left its traces in the hearts of many. To that degree you and I share common humanity with Bob Heller and, to that degree, we are not strangers and I am perhaps closer to him than I think. I can resonate with that life, gone, but not gone entirely.

But, of course, as I suggested, we share something else beyond the common human journey. We share the priesthood of Jesus Christ. Our mutual life in the priesthood has taken us though five popes, one ecumenical council, and the heady and dissonant aftermath in both church and society that hasn't settled yet. We started out, Bob and I, celebrating the Holy Mass in Latin and wound up celebrating it in English. We turned our backs twice: once to the people, the other to the wall. We saw a full class in 1955 of 109 young men, our peers and classmates, dwindle to half, as many have gone through death or departure. From the Diocese of Trenton we were thirteen ordained in that cathedral forty years ago, six of whom, including now Robert, are deceased, two of whom have left the active priesthood, leaving five of us original thirteen still active.

That's the physical parameters of the priesthood we shared. But with all the upheavals, big and small, there was one commonality: quiet fidelity and steadfast service. Think of his career: the countless Masses celebrated, the word preached, the sorrowful comforted, the ignorant instructed, the poor tended to, the babies baptized, the reconciliations effected, the marital unions consecrated, the sick anointed, the eyes closed, the comfort given, the dead buried. Bob's career, his priesthood, his ministrations were what counted, the proof that he *was* worth something, that his life was justified. All this is what we *do* have in common with each other—and with Christ. For the only living proof Jesus himself could come up with when challenged to give an account of *his* life and ministry was precisely and simply to recount:

> *Go and tell John what you have seen and heard:*
> *the blind recover their sight*
> *the cripples walk*
> *lepers are cured*
> *the deaf hear*
> *the dead are raised to life*
> *and the poor have the good news preached to them.*
> *And blessed are those who find no stumbling block in me.*

That's a legacy to bequeath to the world, and one that is descriptive of this man, one that lives on, and one that tells us that Father Heller has not only reaped the rewards of his ministry, but also tells me that maybe he was right. Maybe he picked a name at random from his list of classmates, sensing that *any* of us would know what *all* of us would know, that the human journey is God-touched, that Christ's priesthood is powerful, and that a life given in service has every reason to expect resurrection.

That truth, that gospel, that hope, are what we have in common. I guess that's why I'm here and you're here and that's why he is here. Here, but not quite, for this man of fallible faults and priestly service is now the recipient of those words, "Come, good and faithful servant, enter into the joy of the Lord." Words, by the way, uttered in chorus by Jesus Christ and five excited classmates.

$\mathcal{V}$, the Pilgrim

(LUKE 2:22–40)

This homily exploits the Simon and Anna theme of Luke's infancy narrative.

"There was also a prophetess, Anna...advanced in years...a widow... she never left the Temple but worshiped night and day with fasting and prayer...she gave thanks to God and spoke about the child..."

There was also a prophetess, one who speaks forth the truth, Vi Tweedale, advanced in years—she would be ninety-four next month— a widow who lost her husband and a mother who lost her son, Robert, six years ago. She *always* left the temple especially if there was a bargain at the Acme, but she worshiped in her heart day and night with prayer and gave thanks to God and spoke with her life about that Child we call the Christ.

There's another similarity to a scriptural woman: Like Mary fleeing into Egypt, Vi too left her native land of England when a young girl and brought with her fond memories, her strong faith, and her sharp intelligence. In her ninety-three plus years she had, of course, like many of us, many journeys, happy and sad, winding up, fortunately for us, at St. Mary's, becoming one more memorable and colorful figure for which St. Mary's is noted. She had hoped to get back to England someday to see her beloved brother, Sidney, but never made it. His lovely bouquet of flowers here today is his testimony to his sister.

For those of us who do remember, we can still see her slightly bent figure coming faithfully into church. Like many of her era, she would never think of *not* being here. She sat, if I recall, in the second pew and was not happy with anyone who took her seat. She was, to all appearances, obviously a woman of age, but, as we know, not an old woman. There is a difference. Right up to the end she always made us laugh. She was a remarkably avid reader. For years this little old widow volunteered at Lunch Break to help the less fortunate. Right up to the last, she entertained friends—and attracted friends.

One of the stories I like is the story of when she was at Lutman Towers and went to the Acme and on the way there had a slight fainting spell. Mary Ellen Hintz and her daughter spotted her and they swung around again to see if Vi needed help. By the time they got her back into her apartment Vi had quite recovered and, as a proper English lady, served them tea and, as the saying goes, the rest is history. They became friends and Mary Ellen, like some of you, took her all over: to my neck of the woods; to the Manasquan inlet watching the boats come in and out, with Vi recalling stories of her childhood; recently to the Holmdel Park Christmas display; and, forever and ever, shopping at the Acme.

When finally she wound up for the past four years at the nursing home, God sent her a roommate, Ida Hall, a woman as mentally alert as Vi and they became not only fast friends, but enjoyable companions who made life in the home actually pleasant for themselves and for others. And then she died.

This is but the barest sketch of a woman who, we say, was born abroad, came to America, lived here, and expired in a nursing home. But what we're really celebrating here in this liturgy is a pilgrimage of a soul who has at last gone home. And it is, thankfully, an oft-repeated story, the story of quiet faithful people who, like Anna of our gospel, give thanks and speak of better things with their lives and charity.

What we're really celebrating here are the Vis and Annas of our world, flawed as they may be, who keep the light burning in a dark world, the little faithful Temple people who make differences, the Child-worshipers who anchor us all in terrible times of moral chaos and displacements. It's people like Vi—and you here today (and it is important that you know this)—who are the seeds of life. Vi didn't quite make the millennium, but who and what she was—and who and what you are—will make the millennium better. What more can you ask of a person?

So what I am saying is that we are not just remembering and burying an old friend. We are celebrating a prophetess, a life with imperfections and sorrows, but a steady, faithful life for all that. One who lived among us, helped us to define ourselves, and showed us the way. Like Old Simeon and old Anna, she has now received her reward: She too has at last looked into the face of Christ and the words of Scripture are now her words: "Now, Master, you may let your servant go in peace according to your word, for my eyes have seen your salvation." Amen.

John, Before His Time

(MARK 15:33–39)

I witnessed the marriage of John and Roberta and then, almost a dozen years later John got a brain tumor and died leaving his wife and small child behind. The motif here is Mark's stark gospel counterbalanced with a little humor at the end.

I, who with a light heart presided here almost eleven years ago—it was September 3, 1993, to be exact—to witness the vows of John and Roberta, have returned today with a very heavy heart to preside at John's funeral. As a homilist then and now, I have a job to do. A homilist, as you know, must break open the word of God to the occasion and I must say that finding a word to break open was, in John's case, all too easy. It was easy to know instinctively what Scripture to pick. What else but, as you heard, a section of the passion narrative from the gospel of Mark.

Why Mark? Because Mark gives us a picture of Jesus being systematically stripped away of everything: clothes, friends, blood, dignity, consolation, life itself. Stripped little by little, minute after minute, hour after hour, till nothing was left.

But there's more. Intriguingly, there is an ancient legend connected with Mark's stark account. The legend says that the dying took so long—the torture, the carrying of the cross, the crucifixion, the horrible three-hour agony—and Jesus knew the pain it was causing so many, especially his mother. So at the end of the three hours, the legend says, he searched out her eyes among the crowd to ask permission to die. She, knowing that it had to be, nodded. Satisfied, he let out his cry, his last words, "It is finished!"

Then he was then taken down from the cross, from his bed of pain, and placed in the arms of that same mother. And so we have the *Pietà*, humanity embracing its dreaded enemy, death, and wondering if this is all there is. Finally, however, in that sad embrace, Mary too had to repeat her Son's words, "It is finished," and let him go. She had to let others take him and put him away, out of sight if not out of mind.

And the moment he was laid in the tomb and the stone rolled in place, the legend goes on to say, a strange thing happened. Both Jesus *in* the tomb and Mary *without*, and all the others who were there, in a kind of Greek chorus shouted together with relief, "It is finished! It is finished!"

> *They had watched so long,*
> *cried so often,*
> *comforted so frequently,*
> *agonized so deeply,*
> *journeyed so far,*
> *prayed so hard,*
> *spoken so much,*
> *until they were exhausted.*

Until death just *had* to be, because behind its release was blessed peace. For Jesus. For Mary. For friends. For all on that hill of Calvary, "it is finished." But, as they were to learn, not quite.

What a remarkably personal gospel for John, for Roberta, and his family! How it fits!

First, for John, just like Jesus—both about the same age when they died—everything was slowly stripped away. Seventeen months ago this young husband and father, housing manager, hockey enthusiast, music lover, competitive golfer—ask his brother—received the dreaded news of a brain tumor. For seventeen months he and Roberta, and little Sal in his own way, and his family and in-laws confronted the sickness, its ups and downs, its alternating times of hope and despair. Months of operations, doctor and hospital visits, medications, sickness, confinement, incapacity, loss. Loss of facile movements, at times loss of recognition, identity, and control. Like Jesus on Calvary.

All during this time his family watched, suffered, laughed, comforted, journeyed, prayed, and prepared. More than that. They tried to make life as normal as possible and continued to celebrate its daily rhythms. They even, for Sal's sake, threw him a birthday party last week, even though John was unaware of what was going on. They arranged for Father Ed to come and confirm him, something he dearly desired.

They did all they could and continued to do what they could amidst hope and prayer, all the while ultimately recognizing that, standing daily on John's hill of Calvary, death simply *had* to be.

And so there came a point, as it were, when the gospel legend of Jerusalem had to be replayed in Colts Neck, when John and Roberta and his family and friends and had to search out each other's eyes and nod permission to die. They gave it freely.

John said his "It is finished." He had let go. He died on his birth day and birthed his death day. His family and friends who were with him, surrounding him with prayers and love, had let go. And, finally, at this community liturgy, like Mary of the *Pietà*, we cradle John in our collective arms for the last time and then we too will let him go. We all chorus, "It is finished."

But not quite, any more than it was on Calvary because, in the Jesus story, remember, something else happened. For at the precise moment of his total emptiness, Mark's gospel suggests, Jesus was raised up to a new life. Like the seed which in its moment of death begins to sprout, so was it for Jesus. The grave was his seeding place. The love in Jesus' heart was too strong. Death could not hold him. And so there was a resurrection for Jesus and for all who believe in him. And then, as day follows night, rejoicing. Why rejoicing? Because death, dear friends, dear John, had been defeated and always would be. And that was something to laugh about.

A family went to Easter Mass and on the way home, the husband and wife were in the front seat and the six- and twelve-year-olds were in the back seat. The twelve-year-old brought up a question. "You know, we celebrated Jesus rising from the dead. I wonder when he rose from the dead and came out of the tomb, what was the first thing he said?"

The parents said, "Gee, we don't know. That's an interesting question: 'What was the first thing Jesus said rising from the tomb?' We don't know. It's a great question. Let's go back and ask the pastor because we have a smart pastor." (Pastors were smarter in those days.)

They got to the pastor and they asked him and he said, "I really don't know. I don't think anybody knows. But we're lucky. The bishop of the diocese is here today. The bishop is a very smart man and we'll go ask him." (Bishops were smarter in those days.)

And they went to the bishop and said, "When Jesus rose from the dead, does anybody know what his first words were? What was the first thing he said?"

The bishop said, "I don't know. I don't think anybody knows. It's not in the Bible. No one was there."

At this point, the six-year-old speaks up and he says, "Wait a minute. I know what he said." They looked at him. "I know exactly what Jesus said when he came out of the tomb." They said, "You do? What did he say?" "When Jesus came out of the tomb he said, 'Ta-da!'"

That's a distinctively Christian story: for the moment we moved together from sadness to laughter, aridity to fullness, isolation to community. In a word, from a full tomb to an empty one. Our laughter is Jesus' promise that it will be longer than a moment.

The story also helps us to focus on the positive side of John's scatttered graces, the legacies he left us. There is his enduring love for Roberta and the fruit of their love, Salvatore. There are the loving services he evoked from Roberta's siblings: Luke, Elena, Jeanine; and his parents, Susan and Tom; and his two brothers and his in-laws, Linda and Bob. There is the support and service he drew from the unique community of St. Mary's. There are his doctors, nurses, and hospice caregivers who were made even more gracefully splendid by their compassion and care of John. John brought out the best in them all.

Finally, we might say, John gave us the gift of holy relief. His suffering is ended and on one level so is ours, our anxious, daily vigil. Sad as we are, we are glad to see him go into that place where there are no more tears, only brightness, fullness, and the endless embrace of God. Life has been given to John and, as Jesus promised, given abundantly. For there indeed is Jesus who no longer says, "It is finished," but who says, "I make all things new again."

Let me end with another smile by quoting a cemetery epitaph. On a tombstone are inscribed these words:

> *Remember, man, as you walk by*
> *As you are now so once was I.*
> *As I am now, so shall you be.*
> *Remember this and follow me.*

To which some wit replied by scribbling underneath:

> *To follow you I'll not consent*
> *Until I know which way you went.*

Faith tells us that we know which way Christ went. We know which way John went. We miss him terribly, grievously, deeply, but were privileged to help his journey and to have been blessed by his.

It is finished. It has just begun.

Pat, Making Ready the Way

This homily offers a nod to the Advent season and the context of some words (transferable to other similar situations) of author Stephen King. Pat was a beloved secretary at a local Catholic High School who died in a car accident and I wanted my words to nudge the high school kids as well as the adults.

"John the Baptist appeared preaching in the desert of Judea and saying, 'Repent, for the kingdom of heaven is at hand...produce good fruit as evidence of your repentance...for the tree that that does not bear good fruit will be thrown into the fire.'"

This is the gospel, as you might recognize, from this past Sunday. When I preached it I started out by saying, "Ho hum, we mentally tell John we've heard it all before." But wait a minute, I went on. I recall that at Vassar College graduation this year—to those young folk with the world at their fingertips, those privileged people who will shortly be running the globe—our country's most successful and popular writer, Stephen King, spoke. And you know what? Still recovering from a serious automobile accident, he sounded, in his own way, very much like John the Baptist in today's gospel, putting a modern spin on John's words. John the Baptist and Stephen King, it seems, have spanned the centuries and joined forces. Anyway, this is what Stephen King, sounding like John the Baptist, said to the graduates:

What will you do? Well, I'll tell you one thing you're not going to do, and that's take it with you. I'm worth I don't exactly know how many millions of dollars. I'm still in the third world compared to Bill Gates, but on the whole I'm doing okay and a couple of years ago I found out what "you can't take it with you" means. I found out while I was lying in the ditch at the side of a country road, covered with mud and blood and with the tibia of my right leg poking out the side of my jeans like the branch of a tree taken down in a thunderstorm. I had a MasterCard in my wallet, but when you're lying in the ditch with broken glass in your hair, no one accepts MasterCard....

We all know that life is ephemeral, but on that particular day and in the months that followed, I got a painful but extremely valuable look at life's simple backstage truths. We come in naked and broke. We may be dressed when we go out, but we're just as broke. Warren Buffett? Going to go out broke. Bill Gates? Going to go out broke. Tom Hanks? Going out broke. Steve King? Broke. Not a crying dime. And how long in-between?

How long have you got to be in the chips?...Just the blink of an eye. Yet for a short period, let's say forty years, but the merest blink in the larger course of things, you and your contemporaries will wield enormous power....Of all the power which will shortly come into your hands gradually at first, but then with a speed that will take your breath away, the greatest is undoubtedly the power of compassion, the ability to give. We have enormous resources in this country, resources you yourselves will soon command but they are only yours on loan. Only yours to give for a short while....

Not that long ago, we would have dismissed first-century John the Baptist and twenty-first-century Stephen King as full of rhetoric, if not something else. But since the World Trade disaster on September 11, the crash of American Airlines flight 794 on November 12, fears of terrorism and wars in Afghanistan and in Israel, we're not so ready to do that, are we? The current Advent theme of repentance, of making ready for a Savior through the works of compassion while we have time comes closer to home. In our brief time on earth, as King put it, it's up to us—it's our calling—to make ready the Lord's coming in grace, love, and service.

Why this long homiletic preamble? Because it was easy, so easy, for me to think of Pat Costigan on reading this gospel and preaching those words. She, taken in the blink of an eye, *was* ready, for, simply put, she was an Advent person, always preparing the way of the Lord for *somebody*: her children, her grandchildren, her neighbors, her many friends, the staff and students at St. John Vianney. Her family, for example, for which she lived, came first. I knew that. She was Christmas shopping for them just last week, buying for them things she could not afford, but, as she typically said, "What the heck; it's Christmas." She was knitting hats for the grandchildren. That kind of thing.

This was a woman who had her priorities straight: God, family, friends, and job, and it showed in her optimism and her wonderfully quick smile. I cannot help but think that it surely must have been a comfort for students at St. John's to encounter that smile when they walked into the office. She was a strongly faith-filled person and one of the *least* materialistic and *most* down-to-earth persons I knew, utterly without guile. Her life was as open a book as the lunch on her clothes.

When I heard of her tragic death, and almost witnessed it—I was waved around the accident by the police not knowing who it was—for some reason I instinctively thought of her Irish counterpart, someone very much like her: Father Mychal Judge, the New York City Fire Department chaplain, and I remembered the wondrous eulogy transmitted worldwide at his funeral service. This heroic priest, like Pat, also lost his life suddenly. You recall that he was killed while administering the last rites to a dying firefighter at the World Trade Center. In tribute to this fallen hero, the eulogist beautifully pointed out that at his final moments, Father Mychal Judge was 1) where the action was, 2) praying, 3) talking to God, 4) serving his fellow human. The eulogist then added wistfully, "Can anyone think of a better way to die?"

I thought to myself: That's Pat. Those words fit her perfectly. She was always where the action was: at home, neighborhood, school, church. She prayed with us and often talked to God. I would frequently see her at church. We would hug, she would smile and say everything's great. And she certainly served others: her family, friends, and the principals and students at St. John Vianney. A good woman, a smiling lady, even when at times there was little to smile about, who bore life's burdens and joys with deep faith, she was prepared. Death caught *us* off guard, not her.

As a sign of that, I want to share something with the family. As I was being detoured around the block at the accident scene, a woman, Dottie Voorhees, who comes to daily Mass, happened to be walking to church that fateful day. The accident happened right in front of her. She saw a gentleman go over to Pat, apparently asking her something. Pat nodded and then she, quite peacefully, laid her head back and closed her eyes. And that was all. The woman who witnessed this stood there all the while and prayed long and deeply for Pat, and finally, unable to continue to church, went back home. I mention this because I want the family to know that, at the precise hour of tragedy, there also was a pray-er present, one who did not let Pat Costigan make the transition alone but, like an angel in disguise, was there standing by to commend her to God. Chaos was present and police and ambulance personnel and first aid folk, but I wanted you to know that, at that exact moment, prayer was deeply present; spirit, love, compassion, and commendation were there. God had provided for his good and faithful servant. For all the distress in your hearts, cherish that scene.

Finally, I want to go back to Father Judge because he offers another comparison: His, as you may know, was the first recorded death from the disaster and there remains, you might recollect, that vivid image of his being carried from the rubble by distraught, determined rescue workers. His body is slumped in a chair, carried by two strong, dirt-covered men and followed by others. They brought him to a nearby church, processed up the aisle, and laid him before the altar, and covered him with a white alb. His earthly life spent, they presented him before the Lord.

I just want to remind you that, today, here, liturgically, we are doing the same thing. Pat spent her earthly life by preparing for her death, and we have brought her to church, processed up the aisle, laid her before this altar, and covered her with a white cloth. What we also are doing here—with tears and love, grief, and faith—is presenting Pat Costigan before the Lord: like Father Judge, a sudden but pleasing and very worthy gift, quite as heroic in her own way.

May this Advent woman rest in peace. May she who prepared the way for others find a place prepared for her. May her intercession bless us on earth. May her smile add to the brightness of heaven. Amen.

Sally's Birth-day

(LUKE 24:13–35)

Here the outline is that of the Emmaus story but it is en-
riched with theological reflections and literary allusions.

When St. Luke sat down to write this gospel story, it was not just a
fancy and interesting telling of a post-resurrection tale. He was writing for his community, and like so many other communities, it had
to face the question of death. And with death, the feeling of isolation and alienation and shattering distress. And in the story Luke
proposed a number of things for his parish congregation of his time
and for our community, in our time. He's got wrapped up in his story
three elements as to how and why and where a community can find
its own inner healing when faced with death, as the first one was
faced with the death of its leader, Jesus Christ.

Notice the first element: Scripture. When these excited and distressed and grieving disciples were excitedly talking on the way to
Emmaus, the stranger approached, and after their dialogue, what did
he do when he heard the news of their distress, anxiety, and hurt? He
opened up the Scripture. And Luke is saying, in effect, in your grief,
facing death, that's the first step to healing—open up the Scripture.
And so we open it and as we cast our eye here and there, what is it
we read? We read of Jesus standing there saying: "I am the resurrection and the life; he who believes in me shall never die." Or again,
"The one who would save his life will lose it, but the one who loses
his life for my sake shall find it." Or, "Just as the seed is planted in

the ground, if it remains on the ground, it is sterile; but if it is planted deep, it springs up with fruitful blade. So shall I be planted in the earth and rise up again." And so shall you, by implication.

And again in Scripture, "Though your sins be as red as scarlet I will make them as white as snow." Or yet, in Jeremiah, "Behold, tell the people I have loved you with an everlasting love." And so as we review all of these things we turn to Scripture and we see the basis of what we are celebrating today—the death of someone we have known and loved. And through the words of Scripture, we can celebrate in hope because Jesus is the resurrection and the life, and Sally believed in him. And all those who believe will be raised up on the last day.

And because of that we take our tears and our sorrow, and we mingle them with hope and even with joy. And that's why, from the very beginning, Christians have always caught that double feeling about death: the very human tears at losing someone we have known and loved, and yet that very distinct undercurrent of joy. And the church picks that up in its liturgy, and you notice, for example, that we have flowers that we usually associate with joyous times. And we are wearing the white vestments that we associate with weddings. And in the early church, if they had had newspapers, the headline for Sally Gassert would have been: "Sally Gassert Celebrated Her Birthday on the Day of Her Death." Because in the old days, they considered the day you died your birthday, when you were really born again, when, without encumbrance and without obliqueness, directly face to face, as Paul says, you would look on the vision and the face of the Father. And all because Scripture opened up to us the meaning of life and death in Jesus.

The second element that Luke gives for healing the community is one that Sally knew very well—and we know here. How did they recognize Jesus? They recognized Jesus in the breaking of the bread. And as people go through their anger, understandably, and as people are caught face to face with death—death of little children, innocent people, teenagers being killed instantly, the long pain of cancer for Sally—and as we scream and rant and rave and wrestle with these things, and get angry with God, we still find the answer, and Jesus, and healing in the breaking of the bread. And we remember that when we celebrate our Eucharist. Jesus said, "I'm going to take my body and make it food, so this bread can be broken and given; and my blood will be distributed for the forgiveness of sins." And all of us who approach death with our tale of folly and sin know Jesus has been broken for us; and the moment that we thought was doom and destruction and despair—lo and behold—we discovered him in the breaking of the bread.

And every time we in the Christian tradition here meet around the altar and celebrate the Eucharist, we celebrate the life, death, and resurrection of Jesus, and our own life, death, and resurrection—and we discover his presence there. Sally, who received communion everyday from the hands of her relatives, knew what it meant, and how important that Eucharist was—to discover Jesus.

The final element that Luke gives us is community. You notice at the end of that story, the first thing the disciples did when they got the good news and recognized Jesus, they went back to the community at Jerusalem. And here's the final point to healing: the community, the community of the church, the community of this parish, the community of one's family and friends. And it is only in this community that we exchange our hurts and exchange our pains, and exchange our faith, and exchange our hope, and exchange our love, and then healing takes place.

We look around this community gathered here, and we know some of you from this parish have tasted death—some of you have lost little children; some of you have lost your spouse; many of you have lost your parents. And you and I who have been through these things, we're gathered here to share with one another, and to heal one another by our presence, by our scars, and by our faith. It is in this community that we find renewed meaning. It is in this community that we find a wider family than our biological family. It is in this community of faith that we are restored, and eventually you know what happens. It's what happens to some of you. We become "wounded healers" ourselves. So deeply wounded by death and hurt and pain and sickness, we get that grace-filled power that, next year this time, when someone else faces death, we have the words to say, and the heart to give, and the healing to offer because, like Jesus, we've got five wounds in our heart and our bodies, and we're able to touch each other in a dimension we were not able to do before, when we had not known pain and death. And the community makes that possible.

The community, like the family, also accepts us as we are: our good and our bad, our cleverness and our stupidity. And so Luke has revealed to us in this gospel a scenario for what we are about today. We will be healed through Sally's death, through Scripture, through the Eucharist, and through community. Sometimes at funerals we don't talk much about or praise the person who had died, and that is because the funerals, in a sense, are for our benefit—for the living— because you and I have yet to undergo this experience, and someone's death prepares us for it. And whether we are a Catholic, Protestant, Jew, or atheist, none of us can fail to be moved at this.

Sally was prepared more than usual by Scripture, because every day she read it. She kept her wits about her, her intelligence and her humor. A couple of days before she died, at a time when some thought she might be very close to death, I went over to see her and I read Scripture. She had a favorite passage from Ecclesiastes, and one of the other people there got up and read that. Even in her sickness she said, "that was lovely, but it was the wrong reading." And I was there the next day to anoint her with the sacrament of the sick, and we had a long private talk together—very fruitful and very beautiful. Some of the things I can share. She said, "Do you think—you know— what does it feel like to die?" I said, "Sally, I've never been through it; I don't know. The only thing I can tell you is what I read about Oscar Wilde. When he was dying, on his deathbed, he opened his eyes and looked around and said to the people gathered around the bed, 'Well, if this is dying, I don't think much of it.'"

She smiled at that because Sally was a literary buff. She said, "Do you think I'm dying?" I said, "Sally, I don't know; I think you probably are. Yet on the other hand, I've seen people suddenly get cured and get better, too. However," I said, "knowing you, you're a very private person, like myself, and probably if you had the choice, if you got well and were walking around in full health, you'd be a living miracle. And people would be coming up, touching the hem of your garment, and you'd get all kinds of publicity." I said, "Knowing you, you'd probably rather die." And she said, "Yes, I would."

I came over to give her Flannery O'Connor's letters, *The Habit of Being*. She already had it, much to my delight, because I wanted to give the book to someone else, really; and I told her that. Flannery O'Connor, as many of you know, was a Catholic writer who was ill and died of her sickness—and like Sally had to use a walker and two of those aluminum canes when she got around (she and Sally were very much alike). And there was one passage from one of her letters that I wanted to read to Sally, and so I said, "Sally, she's just like you. She's a great letter writer, this Flannery O'Connor. She's writing to a friend and she says, 'I decided I must be a pretty pathetic sight with these crutches. I was in Atlanta the other day at Davidson's Department Store. An old lady got on the elevator behind me, and as soon as I turned around, she fixed me with a moist, gleaming eye and said in a loud voice, "Bless you, darling." I felt exactly like the misfit in one of my stories. And I gave her a weakly lethal look. Whereupon, greatly encouraged, she grabbed my arm and whispered very loudly in my ear, "I remember what they said to John at the gate, darling." It was not my floor, but I got off. And I suppose the old lady was astonished at how quickly I could get away on crutches. I have a one-legged friend and I asked her what they said to John at the gate. She said she reckoned they said, "The lame shall enter first." This may be because the lame will be able to knock everybody else aside with their crutches." That's Sally—and I have no doubt that where she is is with the Lord God—and heaven help anybody in her way.

She had enough wit and intelligence right to the end. The day before she died, when I was visiting her, she said, "Did you get the book I sent over, *The View in Winter?*" And I said, "Yes; I didn't get to read it. It sounds great, a lovely nature book." She said, "No, no, it's not a nature book about winter. It's the story about people in the winter of their lives. It's a story of interviews with old people. There are lovely passages there and I have one for you." And I didn't know that, so last night I found the book. And sure enough, unlike Sally, who had a great respect for books, she had marked in a light pencil, a passage for me to read on page 239, I suspected, after she died. And it's a passage spoken by an old man about eighty-three. But apparently this must have expressed her thoughts somewhat since she took the trouble to mark it for me.

And here is an old, old man speaking: "If I find no home any longer in this world, it is because God has been withdrawing me, my love, my treasures, my remembrances, my hopes, from a place where the frost-wind of death touched every precious thing, where no good can last; but night falls, and only icy solitude and silence remain. This is no home, this is but a lodging." This old man, by the way, was also completely deaf, and all of his senses were leaving him when he said this: "God is making all things dark and silent around me....I must begin to long for home. I seem almost asleep, but my heart is awake... memories sleep, thoughts sleep, but love is awake. It does not think or plan or labor to remember, but it loves. It is withdrawn from the surface of my life to the center....My God, I would not die as the unconscious things—the frozen sparrow under the hedge, the dead leaf whirled away before the night wind."

I think Sally meant that very personally and God heard her prayer. She did not die as the unconscious things, and she did not die as the frozen sparrow under the hedge; or the dead leaves whirled away before the night wind. She died with consciousness, with readiness. She was so much at peace, as the family knows, after she received the sacrament of the sick, and had talked and recognized what was going on. She had made her peace with God, made her peace with the doctor, made her peace with herself. And so she had her community. And I couldn't help but think how again at the end of her life, as at the beginning, Scripture and Eucharist and community were there.

And on the day of her burial they're here again, aren't they? Scripture has been read and rests on her coffin. The Eucharist is celebrated, and community—here you are.

And lo and behold, by the grace of God, Sally has gone up where she began, in front of that baptismal font where she was first made a part of the community, and she ends her days there. She has not died as the frozen sparrow, she has died as a child of God. I think in these words, she recognized herself. And as her faculties were taken away one by one—her ability to walk, her ability to do things—she was being stripped of all the extraneous so she could get at the center—as this old man said.

I firmly believe that in the last hours of Sally Gassert's life, she had found the center, and having found the center, it was time to go home.

Tom, the Music Maker

Again I wanted to take advantage of the Advent season, the time of this funeral, as well as offering a connecting story of interest. Tom was a musician and often played the piano and organ at church. He was also the brother of Sally of the previous homily. He outlived her about a dozen years.

"John the Baptist appeared preaching in the desert of Judea...It was of him that the prophet Isaiah had spoken..., 'A voice of one crying in the desert, Prepare the way of the Lord...' John wore clothing of camel hair...his food was locusts and wild honey..."

The Christian world, as you know, is right now celebrating the season of Advent, a time of yearning, of longing, of desire, of hope. Its chief figure, as you just heard in the gospel, is John the Baptist, one summoned to "prepare the way of the Lord and make straight his paths." That was John's job description, his reason for living: a precursor, a forerunner, a preparer for something, for Someone greater than himself. No mean calling.

John the Baptist. He projects a definite first-century image: camel hair, a diet of wild locusts and honey, a solitary inhabitant of the demanding and unforgiving desert. An ascetic. Not one you would cozy up to. Be that as it may, there's no question that everything about the man *was* geared to one object: to prepare others for the fullness of grace, to open their hearts to possibilities. That was John's calling, his vocation, ultimately his glory. I mention this because I want to remind you that there are others like John the Baptist in every age, including our own, others with his same thrust, same mission. They just live at different times and in different places. They have different images and ways about them, but they're there, burdened with the ancient calling to prepare hearts and minds for something more, something greater, something better in life.

Maybe it's the context of the season, but that is why when I think of Tom Gassert, I think of John the Baptist. Does that surprise you? True enough, in many ways they couldn't be more different. John was first century. Tom was very much this century. John was stern and ascetic. Tom was gentle and kind. John was rough and ready. Tom was sensitive and cultured. John ate locusts. Tom ate home cooking. John wore camel hair. Tom wore blazers. John was a solitary figure in the desert. Tom was well known and respected in the city.

But in one respect, deeply and profoundly, wondrously, gloriously, they shared one thing in common. When you come right down to it, they were both preparers of hearts. Both made crooked paths straight and rough ways smooth. That was their life's work, their calling, and ultimately their glory. In this sense, both were prophets. That's why, were I to introduce Tom to those who did not know him, I would not, of course, as did the first-century gospel writer, Matthew, tell the story of distant deserts and wild locusts, but I would introduce him in his time and place by telling another story that tells *his* story.

It goes like this. There is a statue in a certain town square in Eastern Europe that is not what you would ever expect to find there because it's not a statue in honor of a war hero, a politician, a famous athlete, or even a rock star. Rather, the statue is a tribute to a John the Baptist-like figure and here's its history.

One day during the war in Sarajevo, a bomb was dropped on a bakery where twenty-two people were waiting in line to buy bread. All twenty-two people were killed. A citizen of Sarajevo, a man named Vedran Smialiavic, decided that he wanted to do something to mark the death of these innocent victims. He said, "I am a simple man. What can I do?"

Before the war, Smialiavic played in the Sarajevo orchestra, but once the war started everyone was afraid to venture out just to hear music. With no music to perform, he walked the streets near his home and tried to find things to keep himself busy. But when he heard about the bakery bombing, Smialiavic dressed up in his tux and tails, took his cello and a chair, and marched to the site. He sat there amid the pile of debris for twenty-two days, one for each of the victims of the bombing, and played his favorite piece of music, Albinoni's "Adagio in G." He braved the artillery fire and ducked snipers' bullets and went on playing his cello, trying to show people a better way. Try to picture that in your imagination.

So, the statue in the town square is a statue of this musician, sitting on his chair playing his cello. People today often bring flowers to put around the base of the statue, always twenty-two flowers to honor those twenty-two people. He's a hero to them because he made beautiful music among the rubble.

This is *my* take on Tom Gassert, my gospel version of a modern John the Baptist. Before these latter years and recent illnesses sapped him of his energy and zest for living—his heart attack, pacemaker, leg trouble, and all the things that age bequeaths us—this was a man who literally and figuratively made beautiful music among the rubble and prepared hope in the lives of many, not the least of whom was his wife, Anita, and eight children who cherish their private memories and will pass them on like precious heirlooms. He didn't *have* to be a member and then chairman of the state Board of Higher Education, but he took it on to fight for the right, John-the-Baptist-like, to prepare minorities for their place in society. He didn't *have* to serve as a member and eventually president of the Sierra Club, work as counsel for the Archdiocese of Newark, serve on the Board of Trustees of Seton Hall University and countless other boards and committees, except that he felt he could make a difference, prepare the world for a better future, play a sweeter note among the discords of life.

And he played John the Baptist in secret as well. What few know, except those who benefited, was his consistent, ongoing help to individuals who needed it. More than one person has stepped forward since Tom's death to reveal personal and heartfelt gratitude for all that he did for them, for making very rough ways smooth. He has his own scripture in the hearts of many. And, of course, yes, there was *literally* his music. How many Masses did he play over many, many years to prepare us for profound worship? How many congregations did he inspire to prepare them for singing? How many brides and grooms did he send off to prepare them for a future? How many funerals like this did he play at, sitting at that very organ on that very same seat, to prepare the bereaved for eternal life? And, in the interest of full disclosure, how many times did he raise people's eyebrows when they spotted an ashtray on the organ? [Tom was an unapologetic smoker and always had an ashtray on the organ and, likely as not, a furtive cigarette up his sleeve.]

I come back to where I started. There are John the Baptists in every age. Thank heaven. Their noble if unsung task is still to prepare the way of the Lord. Tom Gassert was among us as one of them. This basically gentle and kind man had enough faith to accept his calling, enough hope to play among the rubble, enough love to believe that he could make a difference. I think the best and final thing we can say about him was that he was right and successful on all counts.

May this Advent man rest in peace. May he who prepared the way for others find a place prepared for him. May his intercession continue to smooth out rough ways and prepare hearts. May his music enhance the heavenly choirs. Amen.

Swede, Casualty of 9/11

I repeat this homily from a previous collection because it still resonates with the tragedy of 9/11.

For decades we have seen in the movies and watched on television the horrors of war. We winced as whole villages were burned to the ground, the billowy smoke the only indication that men, women, and children once lived there. We looked aghast at the continuous black fumes from the Nazi gas chambers. We sat in horror to watch the footage of the bombings of Britain, Poland, France, Germany, the Netherlands. Cities, towns, hamlets, great castles, museums, cathedrals all up in smoke. We watched in fascination the death-dealing mushroom clouds over Japan. In *Life* magazine we checked out the photographs of the massive mounds of human skulls in the Cambodian killing fields. And eventually we all began to watch those horrors with a certain detachment, even those who lost loved ones in the wars, as Hollywood turned carnage into entertainment and killings into box office, mass exterminations into discussion panels, and unspeakable horrors into cash receipts. So we flipped the pages of *Life* magazine to see what Madonna was doing.

And, in a way, no wonder. All those things, those terrible, terrible unmentionable things, were "over there" in Europe and Africa and Asia and South America. We were never bombed. We were never invaded. Our skies never saw war smoke, war ash, explosions. Our cities were never wiped out. Our family members' body parts were never scattered among the debris. So we tightened our belts, used our ration stamps, bought our bonds, mourned our dead soldiers who died "over there," but in our land we were free of the personal horrors of war and could never quite resonate with the wild language and metaphors and desperate prose of our allies who walked stone-eyed and ash-dusted amid the half houses and half bodies of their neighbors.

That is, till ten days ago. The unbelievable had happened. America had been violated. America had been terrorized. In the very blue skies of a beautiful day there was sudden black smoke; and where there were two massive towers housing thousands of people—nothing. The halls of Congress were evacuated, leaders were led to bunkers, the Pentagon was airplane-smashed and set afire, airlines shut down, and a continent of dismay and an ocean of tears flooded the land as people simply couldn't believe what they were seeing on TV.

The country was brought to a standstill. It was like a bad movie come true and we're still reeling from its impact. Terror had arrived at our doorstep and we will never be the same; our travel, our security, our innocence will never be the same. Who among us will ever forget those images of the jets crashing the towers, the fireballs of flame, the towers themselves collapsing before our very eyes, the ash-covered streets, the people jumping to their deaths from high windows, the herds of people walking zombie-like on the bridges away from suffocating smoke, the reports of brave people killed by falling concrete: 350 firefighters, 200 Port Authority employees, 40 police officers, 700 workers each from various financial companies, 266 people on the airplanes, nearly 200 at the Pentagon?

And these—it's so hard to say—are only preliminary figures as New York has ordered more body bags for what is to come. These "preliminary figures" are, of course, people: our parents, spouses, children, lovers, relatives, friends with names, faces, and histories, violently and terrifyingly cut short.

It was within this horrific scenario, this national tragedy that Elaine called to tell me that her son—her wonderful son, Swede— worked on the 100th floor of the Twin Towers. They are no more and at that time she was sick at heart fearing that *he* was also no more. The people at the Armory, where they stack bodies and what's left of them, had asked her for his dental records and his comb to check the hairs for his DNA so they could measure them against body parts. She and her family waited in anguished hope, as did thousands of those others pitifully holding up photographs of their loved ones pleading, Have you seen my husband? Have you seen my daughter? Have you seen my father? Have you seen my niece? Have you seen my friend?

Like the psalmist of old they cry out, "My heart is in anguish within me, the terrors of death have fallen upon me. Fear and trembling come upon me and horror overwhelms me. And I say, 'O that I had wings like a dove! I would fly way and be at rest'" (Ps 55:4–6). But there is no rest. At least, not for a while.

For Swede *was* found, his intact but charred body identified, and if the family no longer has to wait for news to come, they now have to bear the news that has been. They have lost a son, a bright, intelligent young man whose business savvy, loyalty, and integrity I remember so well that marked him out as an unusual boy. They have lost this son. As they say, no child should die before its parents. But it happens. And we are here because it did, and we don't know what to do about it except in faith, in our ritual liturgy, try to grab firmly hold of St. Paul's words, he who knew a thing or two about terror: "We are afflicted in every way, but not crushed; perplexed but not driven to despair; persecuted, but not forsaken; struck down, but not destroyed; always carrying in the body the death of Jesus, so that the life of Jesus may also be made visible in our bodies" (2 Cor 4:5–10).

"Afflicted, but not crushed," said St. Paul. And these words came true in a most striking way because several nights ago Elaine, his mother, had a vivid dream. Three, she revealed, were in that dream: First, there was Swede, twenty-six-year-old Swede, looking quite happy. Then there was an archangel at this side. It is very significant who the archangel was. It wasn't Gabriel, the Announcer, or Michael, the Warrior. It was Raphael, the protector and guide of young men. Then, last but not least, was their dog, "Holly," the yellow lab who had died a few months before.

Thus, her dream. If all this sounds familiar, it should. It's right out of the Bible, the book of Tobit, our first reading, the story of a good but fussy, self-righteous father who sends his son to seek his fortune and a bride but is worried that he, young Tobit, about the same age as Swede, is inexperienced and wishes he had a guide to go with him. And, lo and behold, in answer to his prayers, a certain man, who passes himself off as Azariah but who is really the archangel Raphael in disguise, comes and offers his services, promising that he will be with, protect, guide, and bring Tobit's son to safety. Which, by the end of the story, he does. And so the Scripture, as you heard, tells the beginning of their journey: "The young man went out and the angel went with him and the dog came out with him and went along with him."

Thus the three of them: the family dog, an archangel whose specialty is young men, and a happy son. Quite a biblical story. Quite a peaceful sight. Quite a significant dream. Quite a current sign from God that all is well, that, in St. Paul's words, Swede, like so many others, was struck down by terrorist madness but not destroyed.

This is our belief, our celebration, if you will.

So, remember Swede. Remember him in life. Remember him as your son: handsome, confident, hardworking, honest. Remember him as your blood brother. Remember him as your fraternity brother. Remember him as your best friend. Remember him as your landscaper. Remember him as one who made a difference. Remember him as a good listener, a gentle person, a witty young man. Finally, remember him not in the hell of terrorist fire—that was only momentary—but as he is, in the heaven of peace and joy with his angelic guide and his faithful dog, Holly. That a dog should be in heaven is, of course, no surprise to dog owners. They are more surprised that *people* are there. But that's another story.

A lot of young people came to the wake. I see a lot of young people here today, each with your own personal memories and stories about Swede. Many of you, I suspect, have come a distance. How fine, how decent, how noble of you. Truly. You buoy my faith in the next generation. I thank you for that.

But as I end, I want to charge you with something. I want to challenge you to gradually move beyond your personal grief and momentary sorrow. I want you to take this life, what you knew and loved of

Swede, and use it to motivate yourselves to become more than you think, more than you would have been without him. I pray that you will not have *your* lives shortened, but live them out to their fullest, allotted years, and when you are old I want you to look back on this sorrowful day as a beacon that made a difference to you.

In Steven Spielberg's movie *Saving Private Ryan*, a squadron of young soldiers, you remember, is sent on a mission to find one soldier behind enemy lines and bring him home. Most of the young men in the squadron, including the captain, die in the rescue attempt. As he lies dying, the captain's last words to Private Ryan are, "Earn this." Many years later, Private Ryan, now an old man, visits the grave of his captain. As he kneels at the grave, he says, "Not a day goes by I don't think about what happened....And I just want you to know... I've tried. Tried to live my life the best I could. I hope that's enough. I didn't invent anything. I didn't cure any diseases. I worked a farm. I raised a family. I lived a life. I only hope, in your eyes at least, I earned what you did for me."

Young men and women, the best tribute you can give your friend is to earn what Swede has meant to you.

Mary, the Teacher

(MATTHEW 5:13FF)

This homily is aware that Mary is a teacher and the church, in addition to some adults and teachers, was mostly full of third and fourth graders. I felt I needed a story on their level to keep their attention as well as to make a point for them. This is not something you can do often, but here, at least, is an approach where children dominate the funeral. Since it's short I've included the gospel I used, one that plays on the theme of light.

At that time Jesus said, "You are the light of the world. A city built on a hill cannot be hid, No one after lighting a lamp puts it under a bushel basket but on the lamp stand, and it gives light to all in the house. In the same way, let your light shine before others, so that they may see your good works and give glory to your Father in heaven."

"And it gives light to all in the house..."

When one thinks of Mary Laffey, one thinks of light. At least I do. Mary was a lightsome person, quick with a smile, a laugh, alert, ready with a common-sense word or sharp observation. She entered a room or began a conversation and the room was brighter for her being there.

My memories are fond. I met Mary and Jack, migrants from St. Patrick's, Elizabeth, when I first came to St. Mary's several hundred years ago. Jack being Jack soon offered his lawyerly services to the new priest and, then quickly, his friendship, which I deeply cherished for many years. Mary offered her innate kindness and hospitality.

Some of my precious memories are going over to White Oak Drive with technical business (which always terrified me) to ask Jack for interpretation and advice. Two little girls would disappear and Mary would discreetly move to the kitchen-lounge to correct papers, and when we were finished, was waiting with a cup of hot tea and cookies and wise observations that saw the good side of things. It was for me a winning combination: knowledge in one room, wisdom in another. Indeed, she gave light to all in the house.

And not only in the house, but in the classroom. She taught fifth and sixth grade science in St. Patrick's and then for thirty wonderful years she brightened up St. Leo's school and brought many classes to this very church where we are right now. Which means that she taught generations of children who are now sending their children to St. Leo's. And she taught well. She even had the rare privilege of teaching her own child, Maureen, and her grandchildren, Caitlin and Erin. She planted something of her own light in her pupils and so she continues to shine through the lamp stands of their hearts. No teacher could wish more than that. In fact, she treasured a note from our second reader who took the time to thank her so very much for making the language arts alive and meaningful for him.

There are, I observe, some schoolchildren here—as they should be—and some of Mary's former pupils and her fellow teachers. That is very kind of you. But because this is so, I hope you bear with me as I play the classroom teacher myself and translate something of Mary's spirit. And how else, as is my custom, but with a story? It's an old English tale (sorry about that, Mary) familiar to some of you teachers, called "The Hedley Kow (spelled with a K) and it goes like this:

One day it happened that an old woman, Mrs. Miller, was on her way back home from market one day, trudging peacefully through the twilight, thinking of her nice, warm fireside, when she saw something lying in the road ahead.

"Why, it's a pot, a big iron pot. It must have fallen off someone's wagon. Or else there's a hole in it somewhere, and so it's been just thrown away. A good, useful thing like that why, I can use it, hole or no hole, to plant some flowers in."

But when she looked in the pot, the old woman gasped. "Gold pieces! The pot is full of gold pieces! Why, what a lucky woman I am!" Tying her sturdy woolen shawl around the pot, she began to drag the heavy thing home. But something felt very strange about her burden. And when she turned around to see what was wrong, the old woman gasped again.

"My eyes must have played a trick on me. How could I ever have mistaken that for a mass of gold coins? It's a lump of *silver*. Better and better! If I tried to spend all of those coins, folks would wonder where I got them. They might even think I was a thief! No, no, a lump of silver will be much simpler to sell. *Why, what a lucky woman I am!*"

Off she went again, dragging the lump of silver behind her. But once more, something felt very strange about it, and she turned around to see what was wrong. "Now, isn't this the silliest thing? My eyes really are playing tricks on me. How could I have thought this was a lump of silver when it's a nice mass of iron, good, solid iron. Better and better yet! Silver would be odd to sell, and folks would still be wondering if I was a thief, but iron well, any ironsmith will gladly buy it from me. What a lucky woman I am!"

Off she went again, dragging the mass of iron after her. But once more, something felt very strange about her burden, and she turned to see what was wrong. "Oh, my. Oh, dear. Oh, my dear. It must be the dim twilight fooling me, that's what it is. That's no mass of iron I'm pulling along, it's a good, heavy stone. A nice, smooth, round one, too—exactly what I've been needing to prop open my door. What a lucky woman I am!"

She hurried home with her prize and set it beside the door. But no sooner had she untied the shawl from the rock than Whoosh! The rock was suddenly growing, sprouting ears and legs and a long donkey tail. Before the old woman could so much as gasp, the creature was gone into the night, braying and laughing. "Oh, my dear, dear me, that was no stone, that was the Hedley Kow!

"And to think I had a chance to see him. What a lucky, lucky woman I am!"

Children, pupils, new and old, teachers, *that* was Mary Laffey, a woman who always used to sing an old song way before some of your time: "Accentuate the positive, eliminate the negative, latch on to the affirmative, don't mess with Mr. In-Between." A good characterization.

There was, of course, a source for her light. We shouldn't fail to mention that. Besides her effervescent Irish heritage—that was always delightfully apparent—there was her faith. She could anchor the worst news, the worst follies and the worst tragedies there, as she did when she lost her parents three years apart and her beloved "My Jack" five years ago. God was her constant light, the jump-start of her optimism and buoyancy. She prayed and went to church and breathed in and out her faith easily. She lived what she believed.

I hadn't seen too much of her since I left St. Mary's. In the past year I heard that she was sick and when I saw her, for the last time as it turns out, at my Jubilee celebration in September I asked her how she was doing. She smiled and laughed as usual and, as usual, said, "Fine. Things are going well. It will be all right" They weren't going well and eventually *didn't* go well but you sensed the unspoken refrain anyway, "What a lucky woman I am!"

We're the lucky ones to have known her: wife, mother, grandmother, sister, aunt, teacher, friend, believer. She lit up our lives. And now, greeted by Jack and a hundred thousand relatives, and enfolded in the arms of a God she always clung to, she knows how truly lucky she is.

We all have seen your good works, Mary Laffey, and know how lucky we are. Let us give praise to our Father in heaven for what has been, is, and will be. Amen.

Eleanor, Who Did Not Look Back

(MARK 2:1–12)

*Eleanor did not have an easy life, yet her shining char-
acteristic was that she did not spend her life moaning,
"Woe is me!" but steadfastly refused to look back. She
focused instead on the present grace and future promise.
This homily, adapted from a Sunday homily, catches her
attitude. This, then, is a homily for the type of person
who looked forward not backward. The gospel about the
man lowered through the roof is critical here.*

There is one word that comes to mind and comes to heart when I
think of Eleanor Brady—the gospel gave you a hint—and she would
love what I'm about to do to reveal it. To no one's surprise, to get at
that woman and that word and that gospel, I am going to tell some
stories, three of them, that fit Eleanor to a "T." So bear with me. The
first one's in the form of a little allegory and it's titled "The City of
Regret." It goes like this:

I had not really planned to take a trip this year, yet I found myself
packing anyway. And off I went, dreading it. I was on another guilt
trip. I booked my reservation on "Wish I Had" airlines. I didn't check
my bags—everyone carries their baggage on this airline. I had to drag
[my bags] for what seemed like miles in the Regret City airport. And
I could see that people from all over the world were there with me,

limping along under the weight of bags they had packed themselves. I caught a cab to Last Resort Hotel, the driver taking the whole trip backward, looking over his shoulder. And there I found the ballroom where my event would be held: the Annual Pity Party. As I checked in, I saw that all my old colleagues were on the guest list:

The Done family—Woulda, Coulda and Shoulda; Both of the members of the Opportunity family were there—Missed and Lost. All the Yesterdays were there, too—there were too many to count, but all would have sad stories to share. Shattered Dreams and Broken Promises would be there, too, along with their friends Don't Blame Me and Couldn't Help It. And of course, hours and hours of entertainment would be provided by that renowned storyteller, It's Their Fault.

As I prepared to settle in for a really long night, I realized that one person had the power to send all those people home and break up the party—me. All I had to do was, with some help, return to the present and welcome the new day!

My second "Eleanor-like" story is one you may already know, the story of retail genius, J.C. Penney. In the early years of the Great Depression Penney lost a large part of his fortune and the fruits of thirty years of hard work. He suffered a nervous breakdown. In the hospital, which he could ill afford, the fifty-eight-year-old businessman confronted his deepest fears and questioned his most dearly held values. He described later the turning point: "One night I became possessed of the strange idea that the end of life had come for me, and that before morning I would be gone. I took a sedative, and went to sleep at nine o'clock. After an hour I awoke, still with the conviction that this was the last night on earth for me. I got up, wrote farewell letters to my family, returned to bed, and again fell asleep. To my surprise I was still alive the following morning. Feeling restless and apprehensive, I dressed and went downstairs to the dining room, intending to have breakfast. The place had not yet been opened. I wandered disconsolate down the corridor. Presently the sound of singing led me to the chapel, where a small group of people was engaged in an early morning prayer meeting. They were singing the old, familiar hymn: 'Be not dismayed whate'er betide, God will take care of you.'

"Slipping inside, I sat down in one of the back seats. Someone read a passage of Scripture that was followed by a prayer. Silently, yet in agony of spirit, I cried: 'Lord I can do nothing! Will You take care of me?' Something I can only explain as a miracle happened to me In that quiet chapel an appalling weight was lifted from my spirit and I passed from darkness to light. I had entered the room paralyzed in spirit, and helplessly adrift. I left it with an exhilarating sense of relief from the thought of impending death and a reborn hope in life."

Finally: "My drug use began to destroy my family relationships. I remember one day that I had promised my son that I would pick him up on payday and we would spend the day together. Instead of using my check for a day with him, I stopped, bought some 'stuff,' and got high. Another day I even caused my own mother to pull a gun on me because I wanted some money back that I had given her to keep for me. She told me that she would rather kill me than see me living like I was! The drugs had such a grip on me that I still went out and got "high." Upon returning to my room I sat on my bed and decided that Mom was right, that it would he better to die than live this life.

"I toyed with my mother's gun and as I sat there looking at it, the alarm clock beside my bed suddenly went off. I truly believe that this was nothing short of an act of God, getting my attention. As I reached for the alarm I slowly pushed the gun aside. Seeking help, I entered a hospital in Philadelphia. While lying in my bed, I heard a nurse telling another man about a program in Harrisburg, Pennsylvania, that had changed her brother's life! The man she was talking to was not interested in hearing what she had to say, but God touched my heart right then and right there. God used this nurse to save my life! After talking with her, I got on a train to Harrisburg....Now, over three years later, I am truly free! It was the Christ-centered program of Bethesda that the Lord used to release me from the shackles of fear and doubt that had kept me in bondage for so long."

Eleanor Brady is all of these stories. Faced with disappointments, a divorce, persistent illnesses, she refused to take up residence in the City of Regret. With her common-sense verve and her sharp insight, she knew there was a future. Her practical determination to seek that future is evidenced in the manifesto she wrote when she co-founded the Singles' Journey. Some of you remember it well:

"Every Sunday at 11:30 AM friends gather here at St. Mary's for an hour or so of companionship, caring, and sharing. We are men and women who came as strangers and are now friends; we are separated, divorced, widowed, or never married, but find a strong, common bond in our struggles to live a committed Christian life as single persons. Our stories are unique and our paths are diverse, but we share as a common goal a desire to heal and to grow and to seek new directions in our lives....Let us look objectively at the past to learn from it, never to dwell on it...Let us look kindly at the present. May we be gentle with ourselves and each other for we are at different stages in our journey....Let us look hopefully at the future. May we see the wonderful possibilities that are open to us as single travelers, and may we share both joy and sorrow, laughter and tears as we grow together...."

No City of Regret for this lady.

Next, she, like so many others, in her search for God, stumbled on St. Mary's one day. She too, like J.C. Penney, heard "the singing in the chapel" and she was moved and touched by it and decided to stay and her staying made a difference as she moved from ministry to ministry, served on the parish council, becoming a vital part of what makes St. Mary's work.

Finally, moving from regret and having found a community, she became something deeper: she became a certified and certifiable friend. She became to others what that nurse was to the addict: she became a guide, an inspiration, encourager and a collaborator who showed the way to healing. She spent much of her time lowering people who had given up to Jesus.

There is that word again: friend. "Friend" is the one word I had in mind when I think of Eleanor Brady. She was daughter, mother, grandmother, sister, and aunt to some, but she was friend to many with all of the richness that that word implies.

Not the least of all, she was friend to me and I miss her. Every few months we would routinely meet for lunch. Usually I would drive to

Rossmoor where she ecumenically shared her friendship, and she in turn would drive me in her car the short distance to Fiddlebacks restaurant while I would hold my breath vainly trying not to inhale the cigarette smoke that clung everywhere. Ailments increased throughout the latter years and over lunch I would listen to this or that tale of medical woe or incompetent insurance company but always spoken with laughter, witty asides and determination—and pride when she finished everything on her plate.

From Teaneck to Matawan to Colts Neck to Monroe Township, Eleanor Brady was a friend. And now the Scripture comes alive once more. At this Memorial Mass we, her friends, through our prayers and liturgy, have taken off the tiles of memory and lowered her before the Lord. And once more those gospel words are spoken and spoken with deep love and compassion, "Eleanor, rise up. Rise up from your frailty, your sickbed, your medicines, your confinement. Forever Friend, pick up your mat and walk."

Carol and Her Parachutes

*The Lukan gospel of the Magnificat gives me permission
to wrap this funeral homily around another Sunday homily that employed the interesting story of Charles Plumb.
The framework here is that story for similar people.*

The moment I learned of Carol Jones' death is the moment I immediately thought of an old story I think I shared with you before. Allow
me to reprise it.

His name was Charles Plumb. He was a U.S. Navy pilot in Vietnam. After seventy-five combat missions, his plane was destroyed
by a surface-to-air missile. Plumb ejected and parachuted into enemy hands. He was captured and spent six years in a Communist
Vietnamese prison. He survived the ordeal and now he spends his
time lecturing on the lessons he has learned from that experience. He
didn't know it, but he was about to learn and preach another lesson.
It happened this way. One day, when Plumb and his wife were sitting
in a restaurant, a man at another table came up and said excitedly,
"You're Plumb! You flew jet fighters in Vietnam from the aircraft car-
rier Kitty Hawk. You were shot down!" "How in the world did you
know that?" asked the amazed Plumb. The man replied, "I packed
your parachute."

Plumb gasped in surprise and gratitude. While he was speechless,
the man pumped his hand and said, "Well, I guess it worked!" Plumb
regained his composure and assured him, "It sure did. If your chute
hadn't worked, I wouldn't be here today." And they parted.

End of coincidence, end of story? Not quite. You see, Plumb couldn't sleep that night. He kept thinking about that man. Plumb says, "I kept wondering what he might have looked like back then in a Navy uniform: a white hat, a bib in the back, and bell-bottom trousers. I wonder how many times I might have seen him and not even said 'Good morning, how are you?' or anything because, you see, I was a fighter pilot and he was just a sailor."

Plumb then began to think of the many hours the that ordinary sailor had spent on a long wooden table in the bowels of the ship, carefully weaving the shrouds and folding the silks of each chute, holding in his hands each time the fate of someone he didn't know.

So Plumb, having thought long and hard about this meeting, now asks his audience when he lectures, "Who's packing your parachute?" His point is that everyone has someone who has packed their parachutes, who has blessed them, who has provided what they need to make it through the day.

Plumb points out that in fact he needed many kinds of parachutes when his plane was shot down over enemy territory—he needed his physical parachute, his mental parachute, his emotional parachute, and his spiritual parachute. He called on all these supports before reaching safety. And somebody had put them there, had richly blessed him. And he was grateful and determined to pass on that blessing.

A story that makes us ask: Who blessed you this week? Think. Who made your lunch, did your laundry, fixed your car, cleaned your streets, picked up your garbage, took your pulse, opened your door, waited on your table, brought your mail? Who blessed you today, yesterday? Who packed your parachute?

For those of you who knew Carol Jones, you can see the point of the story, the point of the comparison and why I put her and Plumb together in my mind. Simply put, Carol was a parachute packer. Carol packed many a parachute and Carol blessed us and those of us who were beneficiaries now remember that fondly. She wore several hats. She was professionally, as you know, a psychologist. She worked hard to get her doctorate at Seton Hall about five years ago and worked for the State of New Jersey in various facilities in South Jersey for mentally and emotionally afflicted people. And she was a rarity. She made house calls. In her career, she blessed countless people who were wounded, packed endless parachutes, wove the fabric of concern, folded the silk of compassion and held in her hands the fate of many.

Then, when she wasn't making beautiful healing music, she was making beautiful physical music. She was our piano player; ours, our very own. Although growing up in Pennsylvania and Ohio and living in Eatontown, she, like so many others, was drawn to us and for over fifteen years she migrated to St. Mary's. And not just as a passive parishioner. No, she packed parachutes there too.

For years she and Elaine Baran made a formidable team as they coaxed, bribed and cajoled the children into singing those glorious songs that so enhanced our children's' liturgies. She played for that stunning production, *The Great Late Potentate*. She played with and sang with this very contemporary adult choir here today.

When she wasn't making healing and physical music, she was contending, in these latter years, with the discordant notes of personal illness. She bore it well. Occasionally she would email me with her optimistically revealing comments about her work, passing along her jokes—she had a great sense of humor—adding her wry commentary on the foibles of the Church and ultimately talking about her sickness. She promised we would get together. We never did.

Her illness, her cancer, spread rapidly until she died last Sunday. Elaine and Steve Carroll were there. Elaine relates how agitated and restless Carol was, breathing labored breaths until Elaine put some music on the CD player and immediately Carol became calm and her breathing slowed down. Fittingly, the music she made, made her. It was, I thought, a kind of divine parable. The God she honored by her ministry and music returned the favor.

We give our sympathy to her brother Paul and his family and her brother Jeff. We cherish her memory. We call her blessed.

For blessed she is—and blessed she did: this parachute-packer, this healer of spirits, this maker of music, this purveyor of laughter, this friend who has another friend awaiting her with all the kids lined up to greet her.

With them, once more she plays the music. The lyrics now belong to her:

My soul magnifies the Lord
and my spirit rejoices in God my savior.
for he has looked with favor on the lowliness of his servant.
Surely, from now on all generations will call me blessed;
for the Mighty One has done great things for me
and holy is his name.

Elaine: She Was the Gift

(JOHN: SHORTENED AND EDITED
FROM CHAPTER 11:1–43)

Elaine was one of those vivacious, talented women who taught at the local community college, worked with the children at the parish (her signature song with them was "You are the Gift"), presented musical plays with them, sang in the choir, and acted in the adult religious musicals at church. Dying suddenly, she was a free spirit who left her mark. I've taken a familiar gospel and its familiar themes that I have already explored in this book and expanded them to fit her larger-than-life persona.

When I was thinking of this extravagant lady before us,
   grower of flowers and plants,
   knowledge and children;
   this Elaine Bertucci who with Carl Baran stood in this very church
      slightly over twenty years ago, October 20, 1974, for a wed-
      ding—a rather flamboyant one as I recall (but could it be other-
      wise?)—
   whose children Jonathan, Cara, and Therese I baptized in this very
      church;
   this vivacious lady whose mind was wide and international, whose
      languages were several, whose kindness was singular and strong,
      who concocted music and books;
   who taught children to sing "You are the Gift" and in the process

herself became a gift; who could often excite and sometimes exasperate;

who was a humanitarian and more than that: she was a deep believer whose faith informed and inspired her career;

who, finally, was a friend to you, to me, to Christ...

I asked myself what Scripture would be appropriate for this woman and her family who are gathered here this morning and it seemed to me that this famous Gospel story about Lazarus was fitting for it deals profoundly with friendship and, at the very same time, it has the same four identical characters in the story who are also in this church this morning.

The first gospel character is Lazarus. We don't know what he died of, whether it was slow or sudden. Whatever it was, it got to him, and little by little Lazarus became immobilized and in the custom of those times, in the Near East, they began to wrap his body from toe to head with these linen strips until he was quite like a mummy. He died and they buried him. And so with Elaine. Little by little, strip by strip, she got bound: by her stroke, then her second stroke, by the hospital, the medication, the monitor, the life support systems. Each day, each hour you went to see her you could see the linen strip going around a little bit more until finally she died. Lazarus was Elaine; Elaine is Lazarus; same story, different names.

And then the second group of characters is Martha and Mary. Fussing over their brother, running to the sick room; bringing his medicine; weeping, praying, being angry. And so it was with Carl and the children, the brothers and sisters, the family, going to Jersey Shore hospital morning, noon, and night, every few hours. Like Martha and Mary fretting, crying, praying, hoping, wishing. Martha and Mary, the Baran family: same group of characters.

But then a third character enters the story. His name is Jesus. It is interesting to notice how the story introduces him. I don't know what your concept of Jesus is one way or the other. If you've been influenced by the media enough you probably think of him as coming down from Mount Olympus with great shining power. But if you think of him that way, you have no resonance with this story. He's no mighty lord from Olympus. He enters the story as a lowly friend; a friend who loved *his* friend. "And he wept." You notice several times that was brought out—he was moved with the deepest emotions. "And again he wept." Three times the gospel said that. And when the gospel says, "He wept" it's not like our weeping. This is the Near East's expression of throwing your head back and letting out a primal scream. This was his *friend!* He was friend to Lazarus and he was friend to Elaine.

That friendship was forged when she was baptized. In our theology, when you are baptized, a special bond of friendship is forged between God and this person. And at that baptism, God pledges fidelity. We may wind up faith-less, but God's nature is to be faithful nonetheless. And you notice, therefore, that when Elaine was brought into this church, we deliberately brought her body and rested it in front of that baptismal font to remind us that fifty years ago her parents thought so much of their faith that they wanted to share it. And when Elaine was baptized that friendship was forged and now she winds up precisely where she began, and that white cloth over her coffin is nothing more or less than the little baptismal robe stretched wide and long to accommodate an adult. And at her baptism the Lord said, "Elaine you are my beloved, my friend." And today he repeats that. Where his friends are, so is Jesus.

Finally there's the fourth group of characters, the Jewish folk: sensitive, weeping, caring, supporting. And don't we have them here? The confers and colleagues from Brookdale College, the choir members with whom she sang; the parents whose children she taught; the people in the International Scholarship Program represented by Fr. Neill here—all of you from different backgrounds and different shades of belief or disbelief, faith or agnosticism—it makes no difference. Because there's one commonality we have and that's our humanity, our sympathy, and our friendship.

So you see in our Gospel story the cast is in place. We have Lazarus, we have Martha and Mary, we have Jesus, and we have the crowd and all are weeping. But then, as you recollect, the story takes a dramatic turn. Jesus steps forward, prays deeply, calls his friend's name loudly, and Lazarus stumbles out of the tomb wrapped in his linen strips, and Jesus says quietly to the others, "Untie him and set him free." And awe struck them all.

How the early Christians loved this story! Now they knew that the love of a friend was stronger than death and that the life of a friend was greater than the tomb. The depth and the freedom of Jesus' love were liberating and could make all things new again. Jesus had authority over death, an authority rooted in his friendship love. And so we continue to believe that. We continue to believe that this same Jesus who groaned loudly over his friend Elaine loved her no less than Lazarus and has said to his angels and his saints, "Untie her. Set her free." Take away the mortality. Take away the fractured and wounded heart. Take away the pain. Take away the intravenous. Take away the needles. Take away the medication. Take away the monitors. Take away the life support systems. Untie her. Let her go, set her free and let me embrace my friend uninhibited.

And that statue behind me and in front of you—Jesus reaching out with an embrace—is more than a statue. It's a statement of faith. And so as a result of our belief, we Christians have a tendency to celebrate that embrace of this woman, this wife, this mother, this teacher and friend. An undercurrent of joy runs deeply beneath our mourning and our pain. We dare to wear the white vestments that are associated with joy and weddings; we dare to place flowers in front of the altar, those harbingers of hope. We dare to put out the Paschal Candle, that Easter sign of the Risen Christ, the Christ who dissipates the darkness of death and cries out everywhere and at all times for his friends, "Untie them and set them free!"

So you see, yesterday's Gospel is today's good news, today's hope. And that's what we're all about here in our faith community. But still—still—even as we enter into the story, even as we believe that Jesus has untied Elaine Baran from the bonds of death, the fact is that we are left with the empty tomb. We are the ones left with the grief, the absence, the anger, the doubt. These things will hurt for a long time. What then shall we do?

Let me close with a suggestion, one that Elaine would delight in. It is a story told to me by my uncle. He told a lot of tall tales, this uncle of mine; he was a character, but I think this one was true. The story concerns the great composer Puccini. You know, *Madame Butterfly, La Boheme.* He contracted cancer as some of you may know early in his career while he was writing his masterwork, *Turandot.*

His friends encouraged him to rest and to stop writing, but Puccini refused, and he simply said to them, "I'm going to do as much as I can in my great masterwork. It's up to you, my friends, to finish it." Well, he did die, and as a result his friends had a choice: they could either mourn and grieve forever or they could do what he had requested, they could finish his masterpiece. They decided to do the later. And so in 1926 my uncle was there at the La Scala Opera House in Milan when this great masterpiece was first introduced. It was introduced by the composer Arturo Toscanini. And when he came to the part of the opera where the master had stopped because of his early death, Toscanini stopped the orchestra. He turned around, faced the audience and with tears streaming down his cheeks he said, "Here is where the master ends." Then a minute later he lifted up his head, wiped away the tears, put a broad smile on his face and said, "And here is where his friends began."

My dear friends of Elaine Baran, you are heirs to her spirit. And if you really want to remember her well, then grow her flowers, speak her languages, teach her students, sing her songs. Remember, her legacy to you, her friends, is the title of the song she taught to the children: "You are the gift."

Helen Huntley, Cloak Toucher

(MATTHEW 9:18– 26)

The images here are twofold: the deceased as a closet contemplative and the role of the liturgy as symbolized in the closing story—a story the homilist might expand further to emphasize the role of the caring community.

Years ago—no, several decades ago—Helen Huntley taught at St. Rose's grammar school in Freehold. I heard that she was a wonderful teacher: lots of patience and understanding. Well, one of her third grade pupils was Bobby Cicero. One day, talking to Bobby's mother, Martha Ann, she asked her if she knew the new pastor who was coming to Colts Neck. What was he like? Martha Ann replied that indeed she did know the new pastor: he had been at St. Mary's in Middletown where her uncle and cousins—the Kitsons and Cornettas—were parishioners and had met him many times. Happily, Martha Ann said, the new pastor was all right.

Now some thirty or more years later it's my turn to ask, What was *she* like, this teacher who wanted to know about me? The answer is that, like all of us, Helen Huntley was the sum total of her relationships. And they speak volumes about her. She was all right.

She was a pilgrim eventually journeying from Little Ferry, her birthplace, to Springfield, to Colts Neck. She was a daughter, a sister, an aunt, an elementary school teacher, a wife, a mother, a grandmother, a friend. She had a son, lost a daughter. She was, I always thought, a gentle, humble woman with a quick smile.

The cumulative lives she influenced in her gentle way are countless—those students who can read and write and count because of her. All those fellow teachers, neighbors, relatives, golf and bridge partners—she was a formidable player—who were a part of the fabric of her life. Her husband, Bill, and son Bill and daughter Kathleen. Helen simply walked through life quietly touching lives. She was, I would say, one of those people who was defined by always being there, one you could count on, no small praise today.

I also think that in many ways, Helen was a contemplative although she would be surprised at my saying that and would be quick to deny it. I mean, her fervent love of literature—reading several books a week—her love of poetry, her love of animals—she even had Muriel Rodgers paint her dog King into several of her paintings—and her love of water all told me that. Close to nature, close to God.

I guess what I'm trying to say is that her life, measured by "The Apprentice" was insignificant and rated a dismissal, but measured by those fundamental relationships that are the essence of life, that force us, with all of its attendant and necessary heroisms, to be truly human, her life was a full and resounding success and rates an acceptance, a gratitude, and a memory.

And now I must add one more piece of identity to Helen Huntley in addition to all the others, that indeed suffused all the others: Helen was a child of God. She was a parishioner, a member of the Martha-Mary Guild since 1967, a believer in good times and in bad, and she had both. She was faithful, and every weekend I would see her and Bill in this very church. Her relationship to God was the anchor for all other relationships. Her faith sustained and nourished her as it supported and encouraged us. In short, she was, as I imagine her, the lady in the gospel: an understated cloak-toucher, a face easily lost in the crowd but, like the woman in the gospel, full of determined trust, and therefore noticed by Jesus Christ, who stopped a whole parade to talk to her, love her for who she was, praise her for her faith, and heal her.

This gospel, I tell you, has been repeated today. She is now whole again. She is beyond the illness that finally and suddenly, much to our dismay and shock, took her. On the other side of death, Christ has noticed Helen Huntley and declared that "your faith has saved you." This modest woman who read poetry and loved people is home.

And, now—now there's the rest of us who are here this morning, especially her family, especially her grieving husband and my friend, Bill. For them words are inadequate, words to tell them of our sympathy, our concern, our love; words that tell them that they are not alone, that there is a community of love and care here to comfort them. How can I convey that in a way they will remember? Sharing a story might help.

Once a woman's happiness was shattered by the loss of her brother, a good man, dearly loved. Torn by anguish, she kept asking God, "Why?" But hearing only silence, she set out in search of an answer. She had not gone far when she came upon an old man sitting on a bench. He was weeping. He said, "I have suffered a great loss. I am a painter and I have lost my eyesight." He too was seeking an answer to the question, "why?" The woman invited him to join her and, taking him by the arm, they trudged down the road.

Soon they overtook a young man walking aimlessly. He had lost his wife, the source of his joy, to another man. He joined in the search of an answer to the "why" question. Shortly they came up a young woman weeping on her front doorstep. She had lost her child. She too joined them. Nowhere could they find an answer.

Suddenly they came upon Jesus Christ. Each confronted him with their questions, but Jesus gave no answer. Instead, *he* began to cry and said, "I am bearing the burden of a woman who has lost her brother, a girl whose baby has died, a painter who has lost his eyesight, and a young man who has lost a love in which he delighted." As he spoke, the four moved closer and they embraced each other. And they grasped Jesus' hands. Jesus spoke again saying, "My dominion is the dominion of the heart. I cannot prevent pain. I can only heal it."

"How?" asked the woman. "By sharing it," he said. And then he was gone. And the four? They were left standing holding each other.

And so, dear family, this community is left standing holding you and we will continue to do so until you are strong again.

Dot Bills and Stephen King

The framework offered in this homily is the speech of Stephen King and the Mychal Judge outline.

"John the Baptist appeared preaching in the desert of Judea and saying, 'Repent, for he kingdom of heaven is at hand...produce good fruit as evidence of your repentance...for the tree that that does not bear good fruit will be thrown into the fire.'"

This is the gospel, as you might recognize, from this past Sunday. When I preached it I started out by saying, "Ho hum, we mentally tell John, we've heard it all before." But wait a minute, I went on. In a speech to the young graduates at Vassar College this year— those young folk with the world at their fingertips, those privileged people who will shortly be running the globe—our country's most successful and popular writer, Stephen King, spoke to them at their commencement.

And you know what? He, still recovering from a serious automobile accident, sounded, in his own way, very much like John the Baptist in today's gospel putting a modern spin on his words. John the Baptist and Stephen King, it seems, have spanned the centuries and joined forces. Anyway, this is what Stephen King, sounding like John the Baptist, said to the graduates.

"What will you do? Well, I'll tell you one thing you're not going to do, and that's take it with you. I'm worth I don't exactly know how many millions of dollars—I'm still in the Third World compared to Bill Gates, but on the whole I'm doing OK and a couple of years ago I found out what 'you can't take it with you' means. I found out while I was lying in the ditch at the side of a country road, covered with mud and blood and with the tibia of my right leg poking out the side of my jeans like the branch of a tree taken down in a thunderstorm. I had a MasterCard in my wallet, but when you're lying in the ditch with broken glass in your hair, no one accepts MasterCard....

"We all know that life is ephemeral, but on that particular day and in the months that followed, I got a painful but extremely valuable look at life's simple backstage truths. We come in naked and broke. We may be dressed when we go out, but we're just as broke. Warren Buffett? Going to go out broke. Bill Gates? Going to go out broke. Tom Hanks? Going out broke. Steve King? Broke. Not a crying dime. And how long in between? How long have you got to be in the chips?...Just the blink of an eye. Yet for a short period, let's say forty years, but the merest blink in the larger course of things, you and your contemporaries will wield enormous power....Of all the power which will shortly come into your hands gradually at first, but then with a speed that will take your breath away—the greatest is undoubtedly the power of compassion, the ability to give. We have enormous resources in this country, resources you yourselves will soon command but they are only yours on loan. Only yours to give for a short while...."

Not that long ago, we would have dismissed first-century John and twenty-first century Stephen as full of rhetoric if not something else. But since the World Trade disaster on September 11, the crash of American Airlines flight 794 on November 12, fears of terrorism and wars in Afghanistan and in Israel, we're not so ready to do that, are we? The Advent theme of repentance, of making ready for a Savior through the works of compassion, as King puts it, comes closer to home. In our brief time on earth, as he so dramatically put it, it's up to us to make ready the Lord's coming in grace and love. To take the time God has given us to daily prepare for a savior by kindly deeds.

It was easy, so easy, for me to think of Dot Bills on reading this gospel and preaching those words. She was an Advent person, always preparing the way of the Lord for her late husband, Bill, her children and grandchildren and many friends. As the obituary said in the paper, "She was active in many of the church's spiritual and social committees." I must say, by the way, I had to smile at the very next sentence in the paper, which didn't seem to follow what went before: "She was born in Brooklyn." I didn't know whether that meant she was doing good deeds *because* she came from Brooklyn or in spite of. Whatever. Although she was taken from us so suddenly knowing not the day nor the hour and death did come like a thief in the night, to use the Advent imageries, she was prepared. A sweet lady, a behind-the-scenes activist, who bore life's burdens and joys with deep faith, she was prepared. Remember, death caught us off guard, not her.

When I searched for other words that would sum up her life I immediately thought of that wondrous eulogy transmitted worldwide during the funeral service the New York City fire department chaplain, Franciscan Father Mychal Judge. This heroic priest, you recall, was killed while administering the last rites to a dying firefighter at the World Trade Center. In tribute to this fallen hero, the eulogist beautifully pointed out that at his final moments, Father Mychal Judge was, 1) where the action was, 2) praying, 3) talking to God, 4) serving his fellow-man. The eulogist then added wistfully, "Can anyone think of a better way to die?" That I can comfortably say the very same thing about Dot Bills should be your comfort, your hope, your pride your joy.

Father Judge's, as you may know, was the first recorded death from the disaster and there remains, you might recollect, that vivid image of his being carried from the rubble by distraught, determined rescue workers. His body is slumped in a chair, carried by two strong, dirt-covered men and followed by others. They brought him to a nearby church, processed up the aisle and laid him before the altar and covered him with a white alb. Having spent his earthly life they presented him before the Lord.

And today, we are doing the same thing. Having spent her earthly life, we have presented Dot Bills before the Lord. And the Lord is pleased to accept the offering of a beloved daughter, faithful wife, patient mother, doting grandmother, loyal friend and giving disciple.

In closing I cannot resist noting what's on a lot of our minds: She has, we are sensitively aware, lots of company. How many valiant women have we lost in so short a time! Walene Luttewitte, Helen Owendoff, Jean Knipper, Mary Vanderbilt, Greta McFarland, Margaret Buckelew, Kay Simone, Madeline Tibbitt, and now Dot Bills—all "active in many of the church's spiritual and social committees." Well, it is not difficult to imagine that now, all together in heaven, they are likewise active. Initially probably someone suggested a Lazarus Ministry, but one of the more sensible ones—Madeline Tibbitt, I suspect—pointed out that since no one dies anymore in heaven, a Lazarus Ministry wasn't needed. So they decided, sensibly, to form a Welcoming Committee—with, of course, Father Judge as their chaplain.

At this liturgy we have made our presentation to the Lord: an unforgettable woman of love and compassion. May she, with her friends, enjoy her peace.

The
Nonagenarian

(LUKE 2:22–49)

This fiercely independent woman of nearly ninety years when she died represents all those who face the transitions of life with courage and faith. The framework here is the passage of history and her likeness to the prophetess Anna who, like her, spanned two worlds, the old and the new. A brief homily befitting a person of age.

"There was also a prophetess, Anna by name, a widow [who] had seen many days. She was constantly in the temple..."

Marie Curran was very much like Anna the prophetess in our gospel reading. She spanned a century. This woman saw the Bolshevik Revolution, the Stock Market crash of 1929, two world wars, the beginning of the United Nations, the Korean War. She was born before the invention of the radio, the car, the airplane, television, computers, and iPods. Teddy Roosevelt was president when she was born. She saw Oklahoma, New Mexico, Arizona, Alaska, and later Hawaii enter the Union.

In reference to the Church which meant so much to her and which she loved and served so loyally even when she disagreed with it, she came into the world under Pius X and saw seven popes, outliving six of them: Benedict XV, Pius XI, Pius XII, John XXIII, Paul VI and John Paul I. She saw Canon Law come to light in 1917 and its landmark revision in 1983. She was born thirty-five years after Vatican I and died thirty years after Vatican II. But for us, most of all, she spent the last quarter of her life in this town and as a member of St. Mary's. How blessed we were!

She brought us wisdom, experience, a determined faith, and an openness that encouraged us to maneuver all the changes in society and in the Church. When she wasn't felling trees, chopping wood, or attending the town's Senior Citizens' meetings she was a vibrant part of bringing St. Mary's from Vatican I to Vatican II. She quickly became a member of the Lazarus Ministry, the Martha/Mary Guild, the Samaritans, the Holy Spirits, and the Morning Group. She went off to Notre Dame to learn the spirituality of aging. She was, as you know, determined and at times a bit flinty. When she barked an order you obeyed. In her eighties she thought nothing of driving to New York or to Arizona by herself to visit her daughter. Her special delight was to speed through the toll booths flipping in her quarter before the lights could change. She had little tolerance for nonsense, a great tolerance for service.

My favorite Marie story: Whenever we had a civic parade in town Marie would invite me over to have lunch first and then I just had to walk down her driveway to get a ringside seat. So the first time I went I entered and she said to me, "Father, just go into the front room and read the paper or watch TV. I'll have lunch ready in a minute." She put on her apron and she busied herself in the dining room. I saw where she had gone, so I went in there and said, "Now, Marie, don't fix up all this. I mean, we can eat in your kitchen. That's where I always eat." But she ignored me and pulled out a drawer in the dining room from a buffet or sideboard or whatever you call it. She took out napkins and linens. She put the cloth on, the napkins on, and then opened her beautiful curio case with curved glass and took out stemmed glasses. She wiped the dust out of them and I said again, "Look, Marie, really, don't fuss. I eat in the kitchen at home all the time." Ignoring me, she went right on. Again I tried, "Look, I mean, after all, it's just the two of us. I really *am* used to eating in the kitchen." Marie then turned around and with that no nonsense gaze of hers said to me, "Father, will you shut up and sit down!" Startled I said, "Well, if that's what you want." Then, I think, repenting, she said more softly, "Do you have any idea what it's like fixing a meal for one?" And, yes, once more the prophet taught a lesson to Mr. Insensitivity.

This indeed is a remarkable woman before us who moved through many roles in her life: nurse, wife, mother, widow, volunteer, pioneer—and friend. For us she turned out to be a prophetess who showed us how to live through life's transitions with faith and hope because, at the bottom of it all, she knew God had the last word. Like Anna, coming on each new scene, each new revelation, she gave thanks to God and encouraged all who looked forward to deliverance. She was constantly in the temple.

In every age God raises up prophets to sustain us in hard times and prod us in good times, witnesses to show us how to live in unsettled times, how to keep faith, how to hope, how to love. Marie was one of those persons. After many years, as it must happen, she became ill and confined. As her time drew near to depart she drew upon Anna's temple companion, Simeon, and made his words truly her own: "Now, Master, you can dismiss your servant in peace; you have fulfilled your word. For my eyes have witnessed your saving deed displayed for all the people to see."

Her eyes did witness much. But so have our eyes. In Marie they have seen the Valiant Woman of the first reading. They have seen the prophetess of the Gospel. They have seen parishioner, lay minister, friend. We thank her for her presence and, like Anna, may she now be looking into the face of Jesus.

Louise Wolf and
John Quincy Adams

This is a short homily that offers a story about John Quincy Adams to frame someone like Louise.

Louise Wolf—Lisa as she was known—was ninety-one, a long life that perhaps makes it harder to realize that she is gone. For most of their lives Peggy and Howie and the children and relatives and friends have never known her *not* to be here. And suddenly she is not.

Not "suddenly" in the sense that her failing health and age were not preludes to this moment, but "suddenly" in the sense that emotionally we feel the gap, the emptiness, the space she occupied in our lives and hearts for so long. She was a diminutive woman. My impression of her was always that of sweetness; there was a sweetness about her, a gentleness, a being-ness that always came through although I knew, of course, she had had crosses to bear and obstacles to overcome and had worked very, very hard all her life.

But, whenever I saw her, she never gave any signs of that; only that smile, the crinkly eyes, the hands that always took mine in hers like I were her son, the soft voice with a touch of accent.

Hers was often a hard life but a good life. And she died like she lived: a child of God. When I was in school, most of us learned by memory that great classic poem on death by William Cullen Bryant, *Thanatopsis*. I can't recite any of it from memory anymore—I have trouble remembering what day it is anymore—but I came across this excerpt that speaks to me of her:

So live that when thy summons comes
To join the innumerable caravan
Which moves to that mysterious realm
Where each shall take his chamber
In the silent halls of death,
Thou go not like a quarry slave at night
Scourged to his dungeon
But sustained and soothed by an unfaltering trust
Approach thy grave like one
Who wraps the drapery of his couch about him
And lies down to pleasant dreams....

She did so live and did so approach and now the divine dreams are hers.

Let me end with a little confession. I never could quite push the imagery out of my mind, whenever I saw Lisa, of that grand old man, John Quincy Adams. She reminded me so much of him. The story goes that when that remarkable American was turning fourscore years, he was hobbling down the street one day in his favorite city of Boston, leaning heavily on a cane. Suddenly a friend slapped him on the shoulder and said, "Well, how's John Quincy Adams this morning?"

The old man turned slowly, smiled, and said, "Fine, sir, fine! But this old tenement that John Quincy lives in is not so good. The underpinning is about to fall away. The thatch is all gone off the roof, and the windows are so dim John Quincy can hardly see out anymore. As a matter of fact, it wouldn't surprise me if before the winter's over he had to move out. But as for John Quincy Adams, he never was better...never was better!" With this he started hobbling on down the street, believing without a shadow of doubt that the real John Quincy Adams was not a body that you could ever enclose in a casket or inter in a grave.

So with this woman and our faith, of course, gives testimony to that. If, as Jesus said, "in my Father's house there are many rooms," with all of the implications of a homecoming, diversity, reunion, and all of the acceptance, comfort, security, and love we associate with the word "home," then as far as Louise Wolf goes, right now "she never was better...never was better!"

Peace, gentle lady.

$\mathscr{Peter}$ and Friends

(LUKE 5:17–26)

This is a good homily for so many like Peter whose family and friends are the real heroes. I've included the gospel here only because it fits so many.

One day, while Jesus was teaching, the Pharisees and teachers of the law were sitting nearly....Just then some friends came, carrying their friend, a paralyzed man on a mat. They were trying to bring him in and lay him before Jesus but finding no way to do so because of the crowd, they went up on the roof and let him down on his mat through the tiles in the middle of the crowd.

When Jesus saw their faith, he said to the sick man, "Friend, your sins are forgiven you." The scribes and Pharisees immediately began to raise questions. "Who is this man who is speaking blasphemies? Who can forgive sins but God alone?" Jesus, sensing their thoughts, turned and said to them, "Why do you raise such questions in your hearts? Which is easier to say, 'Your sins are forgiven you' or to say, 'Stand up and walk'?

"But that you may know that the Son of Man has authority on earth to forgive sins"—he turned once more and said to the paralyzed man— "I say to you, stand up, take up your mat and go to your home."

Immediately the man stood up before them all, took what he had been lying on and went to his home glorifying God. Amazement seized all of them, and they glorified God and were filled with awe, saying, "We have seen strange things today."

I have chosen this gospel not only because it's great drama: the crowds in and out and around the little house, friends appearing with some man on a gurney trying to crash the door and failing this, ingeniously startling everybody by climbing up and taking off the roof tiles causing a surprised Jesus, and the others looking on, to exclaim, "What's going on?" The lowering of the gurney, a bemused Jesus pleased at such audacious faith, the pronouncement of forgiveness, the scandal, the powerful healing, the awe...it's all there.

It is, as I said, great drama. But I have not chosen it for that. I have chosen it because it's *our* story this morning; it's the story, in a nutshell, of Pete Prezioso—and of you and of me. Accordingly, I ask you to note that there are four principals in the story—the very same four being here today in this church: the man on the gurney, the friends who brought him, Jesus, and the awestruck crowd.

Let us start with Pete, the man on the gurney. He wasn't always there, of course. He was a kid, a man, a husband, a father of two wonderful children and four grandchildren, a widower, having buried his wife Marjorie seven years ago, a veteran of the Korean War, a man's man, and a policeman—a *good* policeman for thirty-one years—working his way from rookie cop to deputy chief. A straight arrow who brought out the best in everyone. He was also a generous volunteer and, at church, a choir member. In fact, he absolutely loved music.

So what, let it be recorded, if he wouldn't just let you *listen* to it, but had to give you every song's painstaking history: who wrote it and what year, who played it and where and when—and by the time he was finished, the song was finished.

Pete was a fine cop who saw to it that his officers had a chance to make retreats with the Passionists and keep their spiritual lives in order. So what over those thirty-one years he developed that "cop stare"—I think they give a course on that at the police academy—that made you feel like John Dillinger until you reminded him that you were only playing cards, for cryin' out loud, and he was doing it again and he laughed.

So what if he was impatient with your driving route—he always knew a more efficient way to get there; and so what if his driving philosophy, honed from years in the squad car, was "never look them in the eye and full speed ahead!" leaving his passengers clutching the door handles and reviewing their sins.

Pete was a happy man, a truly and deeply religious man whose faith meant everything, and when he first met Lee on that fateful cruise on the tennis deck, she said that he let it be known immediately, and above board, three things: (a) that he was a widower (b) that he was a practicing Catholic and (c) that St. Mary's went with the package. It was a fateful meeting in the way that an angel suddenly appears in stories. For it turned out that in the short year and nine months they had together, Lee was one of the many blessings that came his way. He would have died far sooner without her. He had developed that hip problem, you know, that plagued him in his remaining days: it was dislocated four times and so he finally went in the hospital to get a thorough going over. That's when they discovered the cancer and told him that had about six months to live. And they were right. He followed every advice of the doctors, took every treatment, but, in the end, he grew weaker and more confined and he desperately needed his friends. He was sick, very sick. The man on the gurney is Peter.

Which brings us to the second folk in the gospel: the friends who carried Pete Prezioso to Jesus, the ones he needed, depended upon. The whole community of St. Mary's, as is its tradition, responded, but none more so than, after his wife, the ROMEOs. For those of you not initiated, ROMEOs stand for "Retired Old Men Eating Out." It's a kind of club where the retirees get together for lunch once a month. I want to suggest to you, however, that a more accurate translation of that acronym is "Retired Old Men Embracing Others" for these are the ones who, like a spiritual SWAT team, respond to every need from cleaning out a widow's garage to taking food to the poor. Naturally, they responded to Peter, one of their own.

Like the friends in the gospel, they brought him to Jesus. They carried him to lunch, brought him to church, took him to the store, visited his house. And in these latter days, when Pete was afraid to die alone, they, with some of the women, took turns staying with

Peter all day and all night long until he died at 4:15 in the morning, dying like the gentle, considerate man he was on September 12, not wishing to distract from the nation's mourning the day before. And, coincidentally, he died when gentle Sil Lutkewitte was keeping vigil, September 12. That was the way Sil was honoring his deceased wife's birthday. In those days and nights, in his constant pain, Pete reached out for the three things that mattered most to him: his family, his friends, and his rosary. They were never absent when he did so. His friends had truly set aside every barrier and lowered him to Jesus.

Then, there is that third person in the story: Jesus. Seeing Pete's faith and the faith of his friends, Jesus has pronounced Pete free of his paralysis: free of the pain, the bed, the medicine, the morphine, the tubes, the doctors, the nurses, the confinement, the fear...free, free at last to take up his bed and go home, a home increasingly populated by St. Mary's folk: Eileen, Greta, Walene, Harold, Rae, Tom...he is at home where the music and the laughter never end.

Finally, the gospel speaks of the crowd: they were filled with awe, the text says. That's us. The sympathetic crowd of family, friends, well-wishers, mourners, fellow officers who so generously came down from New York, parishioners—we're all here, awestruck, to celebrate this man's life, this man who touched us so. We're here in awe at his endurance and his faith. We're here in awe of the spirit of this community. We're here in awe of God for his embrace of Peter, his freeing of his mortality, and his unspeakable mercy and compassion.

This gospel, then, is no stranger. It lives again. Once more there was a sick man. Once more friends have lowered him before the Lord. Once more a miracle has taken place. Once more someone has been freed from the bonds of illness, taken up his bed, and gone home. Once more the crowd, through its tears, "has seen wonderfully strange things today": the goodness of God and the going home of a wonderful man, Peter Prezioso, once one of New York's finest; now one of God's finest.

Pete, may your route be direct and the music glorious!

The Quiet Man

(MARK 12:41–44)

This homily, with its comparison to the widow and its story of the whistler, envisages a type of retiring person, gentle, quiet yet effective.

At that time Jesus sat down opposite the Temple treasury and watched the crowd putting in money into the treasury. Many rich people put in large sums. A poor widow, he observed, came and put in two small copper coins which are worth a penny. Then he called his disciples over and said to them, "Truly I tell you, that poor widow over there has put in more than all those who are contributing to the treasury. For all of them have contributed out of their abundance; but she out of her poverty has put in everything she had, all she had to live on."

This ancient gospel may deflect us from an important point. We rightly hear it as the praise of interior spirituality and integrity, a wholeness of life, a truly generous and unselfish heart. But we might miss something. Go back. The scene shows us a bustling crowd at the Temple, people ostentatiously tossing their offerings into the poor box, the treasury. There are a lot of people to and fro. Yet the sensitive eye of Jesus picks out among the well-robed important folk, a small, nondescript widow—no husband, no son with her in public, that's how he knew she was a widow—and her clothes and her demeanor betrayed her poverty. In short, the kind of a person who could get lost unnoticed in the crowd.

But not by Jesus. He noticed her. No one else did, but *he* did. He called over his disciples, "See that widow over there?" No, they didn't. They were preoccupied with the celebrities. But Jesus saw, Jesus noticed, and Jesus praised.

We are here this morning to celebrate a Memorial Mass for Tread Parker. To remember and to re-member; that is, to reconnect, renew, rejoin his spirit, his legacy, all that he meant to us. In my own rejoining, this gospel episode came readily to my mind when I think of Tread. He was, so to speak, the Perry Como of Colts Neck, the widow of the gospel. In short, was, as we say, laid back, a man quietly enriching lives, softly making a difference, kind and rather gentle with strong ethics dropping unnoticed the coins of integrity and care into the treasury of many lives.

From a versatile handyman who by nature could fix and build anything to an industrial psychologist by trade who designed many management training programs, Tread was also, to no one's surprise, a sometime thespian, a lover of nature, and an ardent advocate—indeed, a crusader—of the environment. Which is why when he moved to Sanibel he volunteered at the clinic of the rehabilitation of wildlife and also took time to speak earnestly to students about their duty to honor it.

You always got a sense that he was comfortable within himself and comfortable with others, and others took him as he was: no pretense, no affectation. With Tread, what you saw was what you got: a man in loafers, slacks, and a T-shirt, an early lover of vintage cars—he even imported his classic Austin Healey to Sanibel—a dedicated "beach bum" with visions of becoming a fisherman, a man who, armed with nothing more than a gin martini and his own integrity, spoke in a soft voice and with the authority of wholeness. The kind who, like the widow of the gospel, could go unnoticed by those who did not know him. But Jesus noticed, and so did some of us whose lives he touched. I have photos of him in my albums of our various get-togethers: Christmas dinners and gift-exchanging at my house, dinner at theirs, the games we played. He's always there in the background, looking benign, adding his comments, a kind of context that kept us grounded. A gentle man. A gentleman.

As I said, like the widow in the gospel, Tread could have gone unnoticed by many, although not by Jesus. The sensitivity that led Jesus to notice the widow and the love that he expended on that unknown woman is but a shadow of the attention, love, and forgiveness he shows us all. Keenly aware of our lowly status, aware of our spiritual poverty, aware of our sins and betrayals, nevertheless the compassion and mercy of Jesus leads him to notice us and offer healing and praise.

So has he done for Tread Parker. Affirmation for what was true in his life, healing for what was broken in his life, eternal fulfillment for what was, as for all of us, only partial here. This is our faith: through Jesus all things have been made new and this is what we are celebrating here today. And it is no accident that today we are here in this church of St. Mary's. Although of a different tradition, Tread often came to Mass here. His strong ethical sense was grounded in belief in God. Now this faith community remembers him prays for him and, yes, notices him. This man, touched by God has, in his quiet way, touched us.

Let me close with a story and the ending of a classic story. In the story, a man tells about the day he was just driving quietly along a country road and suddenly realized that he was lost. He finally stopped at a small farmhouse to ask for directions, and he saw an elderly woman sitting on the porch. An elderly man was working around the front yard, and he was whistling nonstop. The whistling was loud and clear, but it seemed to be aimless and purposeless. There was no recognizable tune, just whistling.

So the stranger walked up to the man and couldn't resist saying, "I see you're fond of whistling." "Oh," he said, "it's second nature to me now." Then pointing to the woman on the porch, he explained that she was his wife, and that they had been happily married for thirty-eight years when she became blind. Coming as it did so late in life, the blindness had been a very frightening experience for her and she was still feeling a deep-seated insecurity. The husband said, "I figured if I just keep whistling while I'm outside the house, she'll have the security of knowing I'm still with her."

In a sense, Tread, the Quiet Man, will always be with you, Mary, and Jonathan, Rebekeh, and Beth—and all of us—in the legacy of decency and honor he has left behind. Tread will always be whistling in the background.

The end of the story that so fits Tread Parker are the final words of George Eliot's great classic novel *Middlemarch*. Speaking of the heroine of the story the novelist writes, "the effect of her being on those around her was incalculably diffusive: for the growing good of the world is partly dependent on unhistoric acts; and that things are not so ill with you and me as they might have been, is half owing to the number who lived faithfully a hidden life, and rest in unvisited tombs."

Tread, may you rest in peace and be forever noticed by the One who has loved you from eternity. Amen.

Madeline, Parish Pillar

This lengthier homily reflects parish tribute to one of those natural-born leaders every parish has (and, I hope, recognizes and utilizes). She used her considerable gifts well both in service to the diocese and to the parish.

I will not intrude on the family's memories or grief. Only they can cherish the intimate memories of what this woman meant to them as wife, mother, aunt, grandmother, and great-grandmother. I can only share the person most of us knew. I can only share my own impressions that are undoubtedly the impressions of many.

I knew Madeline Tibbitt as most of you do, as a friend, and a friend who, it became instantly apparent, was a natural-born leader with that rare combination that all great leaders possess: high intelligence, an incredible, right-to-the-mark fund of practical common sense, and ready humor. In fact, I was acquainted with Madeline long before I came to Colts Neck, never dreaming our paths would cross so intimately. I met her passingly at Sayreville at Our Lady of Victories church, where I would go to visit my friend Father Hafner. That was back in the mid-1950s. She was then president of the parish PTA. She went on to become the Amboy area PTA regent in 1958 and then, to no one's surprise, president of the diocesan PTA in 1960. In was in this capacity that she finagled me to give several talks at the old War Memorial Building in Trenton. And she tapped this many times. And *that's* how we met, on the circuit, so to speak.

She moved to the national scene to become vice president of the National Council of Catholic Women from 1964 to 1968 and she moved to the international scene when she attended in Rome the Vatican Council's offspring, the Third World Congress for the Lay Apostolate in 1967—the same year she moved to Colts Neck where, early on, she became the parish delegate to the newly formed diocesan Pastoral Council.

There was a highlight for her in 1979. At the cathedral in Trenton she received from Bishop Reiss the papal *Pro Ecclesia* medal, the highest Church honor offered to a lay person. *Pro Ecclesia* means meritorious service for or on behalf of the Church. The delicious irony was that by that time, she had been so formed, that the one who *gave* the medal and the one who *received* it had entirely different notions of Church. One was thinking institution and the other was thinking people.

And she knew the difference. This was evident in the way she would frequently come back after attending a conference and tell me, with undisguised glee—by that time we had gained some notoriety—that when she was introduced, people would exclaim to her, "Oh, you're from Father Bausch's parish," and she would smilingly reply, "No, he's from my parish." She had learned her lesson too well.

When I came to Colts Neck in February of 1973 I had no idea I had a ringer on my hands. All I knew was that when I started to try to bring the people together and introduce new lay ministries, here she was ready to lector, be Eucharistic minister, become vice-president of the Martha-Mary Guild, Lazarus member—how often she was up here at so many other funerals—and then I began to appreciate what a treasure I had. We all had. It wasn't long before, given her leadership qualities, I did what so many others before and after have done: I began to rely on her for wisdom and advice and felt secure with her, and so many others now like her, leading others to learn to become Church.

Over the years, she, with Marlene Berestecky, would host the many, many workshops I gave to people from all over the world who came to see what made St. Mary's tick. She along with Carl or Kay

Simone, Dot Boese, Joan Henderson, John Carlucci, Eileen Connair, would even go out on their own, not only giving talks on shared and collaborative ministry but being living proofs that it works.

She was, in a word, a pioneer, the quintessential Vatican II lay person claiming the place of lay men and lay women in the Church and breaking ground for others to follow. And eventually, she, like so many others, like so many of you, became not just a parishioner, but an equal coworker and valued collaborator. And eventually, she, like so many of you, became not just a parishioner, an equal coworker and a valued collaborator, but a friend, a close friend, one you admired and was fun to be with.

She did the full human journey. She took many trips with us here and abroad, and, with her usual common sense, always brought along "holy water"—Manhattans cleverly disguised. She loved to play cards and go to Atlantic City, where she invariably won.

Like so many other victims, I foolishly played *Kismet* with her—her favorite game—and was constantly chagrined at how often the dice deferred to her. (With her usual touch of humor, she bequeathed the game to me.) She and her steadfast friends of over half a century cruised all over the world playing bridge. She had other talents. She was a good cook, made fabulous crab cakes and could cut the membrane from a grapefruit section with the precision of a surgeon.

And—she buried her daughter Susan in this very church ten years ago, January 19, 1991, and last year mourned her brother, an Oblate priest and Golden Jubilarian, who dedicated his life to the gospel in Africa.

After her celebratory eightieth birthday party at McGill Hall just two years ago, at which many of us were present, when she learned of her cancer, with her usual pluck and common sense, she made decisions that would keep quality to her life as long as possible. One of my joyful memories is that, in her growing battle with cancer, I was able to be part of two last, final excursions she was able to make.

In January of last year I picked her up at Fort Myers in Florida to visit the Hendersons in the Keys and she thoroughly enjoyed that. And exactly a year ago in June of last year, still declining and several operations and a colostomy later, I took her with me and my sister Rita to Maine where I was giving a parish mission and she had a wonderful time. I think that was the last extended trip she made.

She was a long time living—a good woman, a faith-filled woman—some eighty-two years. And, as we painfully know, an excruciatingly long time dying. In the final month, how she ached to be released and how we all ached that she would be. We all had to watch helplessly the losses of weight, appetite, activity, control. We all had to witness more operations, more tubes, more medication, more morphine to quiet the pain that we knew—she knew—were but temporary reliefs.

Almost right to the end, as you all know, she was amazingly alert, intelligent, bright, practical. She saw to it that papers were in order, insurances were processed, possessions were doled out, bank statements put aright. She even decided on the menu for after her funeral—and frequently chided me not to be away when she died.

She sincerely delighted in the many well-wishers who came to see her and, although she was hardly surprised, she was deeply moved by the outpouring of the people of St. Mary's from the steady stream of visitors and food-bearers to the volunteer parish nurses, the Hospice personnel. To say the least, she harbored no illusions, welcomed Hospice, prepared for death, and kept faith.

On Sunday, June 4, son Bill called Fr. Ed and myself saying that indications were that the end was drawing to a close. Neither of us were sure she had been given the sacrament of the sick and so I rushed up there and found that Fr. Ed mercifully was just completing the holy sacrament. But she knew us. She opened her eyes and tried to smile when I spoke to her.

I saw her again on Monday and when I spoke to her she flickered open her eyes and weakly squeezed my hand; and then, early Tuesday morning, in a literal play on the words of John the Baptist, "I must decrease; he must increase," she did just that. She emptied herself and let Jesus in. Peace at last.

I have a confession to make here. Early tomorrow morning I am leaving for a week in Maine. Last Sunday at church I prayed to God to let Madeline's prayer that I would be here when she died come true so

I wouldn't have to come back prematurely. "Tuesday would be nice," I humbly suggested. Madeline, always considerate, agreed. We both got what we wanted.

She was indeed the valiant woman and the words of the first reading were never truer: "She opens her mouth with wisdom and the teaching of kindness is on her tongue. She looks to the ways of her household and eats not the bread of idleness. Her children, grandchildren, and great-grandchildren rise up and call her blessed, her husband Bill, for whom this is so hard, praises her. Many women have done excellently, but you surpass them all...A woman like that who fears the Lord is to be praised." And the following line from the reading is our collective farewell prayer to God for Madeline: "*Give her now the fruit of her hands....*"

Madeline Tibbitt was indeed wife, mother, pioneer, wisdom figure, friend. I felt privileged to belong to her parish.

Pete, the Veteran

Pete Casey, war veteran, Irishman, husband and father is the subject of this homily that taps the small home-town motif of an ordinary man. The framework here is the historical genealogical context at the beginning and the Greatest Generation motif near the end. Suitable for adaptation for an elderly person or veteran.

In 1914 Woodrow Wilson was president, Pius X was pope and the Panama Canal, after ten years of construction, was officially opened. The U.S. Marines invaded Mexico, and the Boston Braves beat the Philadelphia As to win the World Series. And Pete Casey was born. He would go on to outlive thirteen more presidents and eight more popes.

Also when Walter "Pete" Casey was born to Loretta and Robert Casey in 1914 on March 3—a month and day he and I share—World War I's "Guns of August" was but five months away from letting loose. Very soon in his early childhood terrible battles would be fought in Europe, and, in the land of his grandparents, Bridget and Mortimer Casey, the Irish Easter rebellion would be ferociously put down by the British. Otherwise Pete's life was uneventful.

After graduating here at St. Mary's in 1931, he got into the milk business with his father and his brother Bobby along with George Keenan—the Raritan Valley Farms it was called, if I remember. In the same year, 1940, that his father was mayor of South Amboy, Pete married my cousin—which explains why I am here—Mary Carini whose mother was a Perdoni, sister to my mother and to South Amboy's Celesta Barbieri and Aunt Kate Nicorvo with whom Mary lived for many years down on George Street.

Caseys, Keenans, Kresses, O'Connells, Nicorvos, Barberieris—I soon learned as a child that everyone in South Amboy was related one way or another, and it was unsafe to speak ill of anyone in that town.

Mary was the light of Pete's life as were his two daughters, Corrine and Mary Loretta, and eventually grandson Michael. They were married thirty-two years until Mary's untimely death in 1972.

Ironically, born during the "war to end all wars," Pete was destined to fight in its second terrible version. He fought in the infantry, the famous 45th or "Thunderbird" division. He was in front-line combat in the war-torn European theater for 220 days with men who became fast friends. He trekked thousands of miles across Europe—France, Germany, Italy—and was part of one of the more poignant events of the war, the liberation of Dachau. One bright moment for this Irish Catholic soldier took place in Italy when, by a fluke of circumstance, he had a private, one-on-one audience with Pope Pius XII. He had more than earned his Distinguished Service medal.

On the home front, after the milk business he worked in the Amboy National Bank till he was eighty-one. He was an original member and founder of the South Amboy First Aid Squad back in 1931, past president of the Lion's club, a member of the housing authority, and had the distinction of being the longest member of the Knights of Columbus—seventy years! That must be some kind of record.

Three years ago, as many of you know, he was Grand Marshal at South Amboy's Veteran's Day Parade and this year he was Grand Marshal at the South Amboy's St. Patrick's Day parade. He was very proud of that. In many ways, when you think of it, Pete Casey was "Mr. South Amboy." And like many second-generation folk in a small town in the '30s, '40s and '50s deep and enduring relationships were forged. So much so that it was often hard to tell lifelong friends from blood relatives. Billy and Joe Keenan, for example, were like brothers to Pete. The O'Briens, Harrigans, and Schwaricks were more like kin than neighbors.

Saying the obvious, Pete was also Irish. Which means that he had a kind of leprechaun look to him and a quick smile even when he wasn't feeling that well. Many times he told us tales of the war and its re-unions, stories of ice skating at the old waterworks and frolicking at the Frog Hollow Swim Club—apparently he was quite a swimmer and ice skater—and he told and appreciated jokes, some corny, some risqué, some topical. For some reason, I recall him telling this one a long time ago. He said: O'Connell was staggering home with a pint of booze in his back pocket when he slipped and fell heavily on his back. Struggling to his feet, he felt something wet running down his leg. "Please God," he implored, "let it be blood!" And Pete laughed harder than we did.

This is a man who at ninety-three still had his wits, still drove his pampered car though he avoided the dusk and dark, still spoke well and wise to us at his ninetieth birthday party, and who had the spooky gift of sitting up perfectly straight in a chair and instantly falling asleep.

But his measure, of course, is more than all I have said. Probably the best, most complete thing that I can say about Pete Casey is that he was, in the now famous phrase of Tom Brokaw, part of "the Greatest Generation." He was it right down to his toes. Which meant that for all his human foibles and failings, he had values. Family was first, friends were for keeping and cherishing, not exploiting, work was hard but it was honest, community—his beloved South Amboy—was to be contributed to, his country, when it called, was to be answered, one's word was to be kept, and, above all, God was to be honored, served, and loved.

Let me share this: the rosary Pete took with him when he went into service was black. When he got out of the service it was brown, worn down to its kernel from constant use. All this is a pretty good description, I think, of the gospel's "good and faithful servant." Jesus must be saying to him now, "Well done! Enter into the joy of your master."

We are sad that Pete Casey is gone but he is glad. He'd run his course for ninety-three years—a pretty good run as he would be quick to say—and it was time to embrace his beloved wife, Mary, and brother and sister and parents, friends, and those buddies of his who, with him, make up the Greatest Generation.

Pete Casey: son, brother, uncle, cousin, husband, father, grandfather, friend, worker, soldier, we salute you. May you rest in peace.

Dick Bertodatti,
Ladder Climber

Here the outline is the fourfold categories of man, son, husband, grandfather, plus the Communion of Saints allusion.

What brings us here today in this church of St. Mary's? The answer is three things: yesterday's memories, today's realities, tomorrow's hopes.

Yesterday's memories concern a man, a son, a husband, a father, a grandfather.

A man. Before all the other identities, before all the other people in his life, Dick was a man who loved baseball. He not only loved baseball but played it well. In fact, his skill got him a scholarship, an "All American Award" and a contract to play professional baseball with the Minnesota Twins. Did you know that? He had that long, lean Joe DiMaggio, Bob Feller kind of a body. There was another love. Next to baseball he loved racing and horses. In fact, he not only loved racing but as a college student he purchased his first racehorse—and it won! And ever since he has had horses that have done well by him nurturing the never diminished hope that someday he would produce the next Seabiscuit.

A son. He was the one and only of Mary and Dominick, their hope, their pride and joy. They gave him a good Catholic education culminating in St. John's University. He did them proud.

A husband. I believe we can say Dick lived what St. Paul demanded of Christians, "Husbands, love your wives, even as Christ loved the Church." To outsiders it appeared that Dick and Maureen strove for "roots and wings" not only for their children but for each other. To insiders—the breadth of respect and love that these two had and continued to have for each other for forty-one years is remarkable in longevity and rich in depth and easy to detect.

A father. Jill, Jodi, and Richard Jr.—all are living witnesses to Dick's paternal care that showed itself with the Bertodatti emphasis on God and education. Most importantly, Dick was a father not only by what he said but by what he did, how he lived. What the kids saw directly and out of the corner of their eyes showed them what a quality father they had and the values they should embrace.

A father-in-law and grandfather. He loved his children's spouses and was crazy about his grandchildren, and his already weakened heart broke at the untimely death of his grandson Alexander.

Humor, laughter, piety, talking to horses, and feeding people marked this man—as did his ingrained sense of religion and mantle of compassion. Such are yesterday's memories.

Today's realities. No matter what our Christian belief in resurrection, there are today's cruel realities. When Maureen wakes up, Dick is not beside her in bed. When Jodi, Jill, and Richard want fatherly advice, they can no longer pick up the phone and ask Dick for his insights on the problem of the day. Richard has become the new patriarch of the family at a much younger age than he would have liked. The grandchildren will never again hear Dick's voice and delightful menace to "get their tootsies." All have suffered a loss for which there is no substitution. Each of us here—family friends, co-workers, neighbors—knows what Dick has brought into our lives and now there is so much he will not be there for: graduations, proms, weddings. Maureen is now both mother and father, grandmother and grandfather.

Such are the memories and the realities. Where are the hopes? This is where our faith comes to the fore. Dick's body will be taken from us. True indeed and tragic—but Dick's soul which gave life to his body is alive. Dick is alive. All of us Catholics, you know, pray to saints. To St. Anthony to find something we lost, to St. Jude for hopeless causes, to St. Teresa of Avila for wisdom, to St. Joseph to sell the house. Why? Because they are alive.

Dick Bertodatti is alive, as alive as Anthony, Jude, Teresa, and Joseph are alive. On Christmas Eve, Roman Catholics in Eastern Europe set a place at table for those in the family who have died. This sign evidences the belief, a certainty if you will, that these persons are still very much alive and involved with the family not only at Christmas but every day.

As Catholics we should be convinced that Dick is in contact with all the Bertodattis who have gone before us, are now, and will be. Our hope in all this is the confidence that something will take place; that, for instance, after today's tears will come tomorrow when we will reshape our dreams and do so with confidence that Dick who is alive, is with us each day and will be in years to come. That grandchildren, present and to come, will hear stories of his goodness and gain strength from his rich heritage.

Yes, we will remember how poor health plagued him after his first heart attack, how he was preparing for a heart and kidney transplant when he died. But we'll also remember his New York accent, his amazing ability to fall asleep in a crowd, his speed at tasks, his ingrained sense of responsibility—that he was a good man.

My own memories, I must add, are of a bright, exceedingly pleasant man and a most precious wife who would affirm me at the parish, support me in the many projects, and invite me to their home to share, over a wonderful meal, joy, conversation, fellowship, and the magical ambiance of Foxmoor Farm. Dick and Maureen were parishioners. Yes but they were more. They were friends, a background, a scent in the air, a spiritual presence that always let me know that all would be all right, a sentiment I share with the family today.

I end with the old Italian proverb that says you never climb higher than the ladder you choose.

Dick Bertodatti chose a very high ladder, one, in fact, that leads to heaven.

Marge,
the Just Woman

(LUKE 18:1–8)

What is offered here are thoughts and a direction for a certain type of parishioner in every parish: the prophet of social justice, the outspoken critic, the activist-contemplative. I reworked a previous Sunday homily for this occasion.

It was the annual celebration at the Cathedral for those married twenty-five or fifty years. The bishop had singled out a Golden Jubilarian, Luigi, asking him to take a few minutes to come to the microphone and share some insight into how he managed to stay married to the same woman all these years. Luigi said to the congregation, "Well, I've a tired to treat her well, spend-a-da money on her, but a best-a is, dat I took her to Italy for the twentieth anniversary," The bishop immediately commented, "Luigi, you are an amazing inspiration to all the husbands here. Now please tell the people what you are planning for your wife for your fiftieth anniversary." Luigi proudly replied, "I'm a gonna go and a get her."

I tell this story for two reasons. First, Marge would have liked it and that alone justifies it. I can hear her short chortle from the back of the church as I so often did when she was tickled about something. The second reason I told the story is because of its theme of unexpectedness. Neither the bishop nor the folk present expected Luigi's reply! We can picture the bishop coughing and two hefty monsignors quickly hustling Luigi from the sanctuary.

But *that's* the point of the story, its unexpected twist, which is the precise mechanism needed to unlock this puzzling gospel with its challenging parable. If you will bear with me a bit, I'd like to pick it apart with you, classroom like, because I think it says something important about Marge.

You heard the gospel: a proud judge who feared no one, neither God nor man, is unwilling to hear the pleadings of a poor and defenseless widow, one without a man, without protection, without status. But she persists until she gets justice and the judge gives in, not out of principle, but because he fears the woman will get violent. It is interesting to note, by the way, that in the original language, when the judge says to himself, "I shall deliver a just decision for her lest she finally come and strike me" the words colloquially mean, "lest she come and give me a black eye!" or, as we would say, "lest she come and punch me out!" Jesus' audience must have chuckled at that line.

In any case, I suspect that all over Catholic Land when this gospel is read, preachers compare the judge to God and urge the faithful, who are compared to the widow, to be similarly persistent in prayer and never give up.

I don't know. I have reservations. This equating the judge with God is very shaky. After all the Bible is full of lines saying that God hears the cry of the poor, that God is eager and willing to give good things to those who ask. So it's hard, when you really look at it, to equate the insensitive judge with God. In fact, the storyline says twice that the judge is not exactly a sterling character, for he neither "fears God nor respects man." And besides—and these are typical Marge Cron questions—is the message that if you badger God long enough you can eventually wear God down and get what you want? Is it right to make God a punchy old man who needs his sleep and if you play your radio loud enough he'll give in?

Is the parable saying that you can bribe or bargain with God? And it really doesn't do any good to go through the back door and say, well, the point is that if an insensitive clod of a judge will finally answer the widow's plea, how much more will God? But that too, I think, is straining the comparison.

I suggest that there is a more fruitful and less obvious and unexpected way to understand this gospel. Why not see the woman, the *widow* as the image of God, not the judge? (Marge would love this!) Once you reverse characters, then a whole new perspective emerges. That is to say that, when the *widow* is seen as a God-like figure, then the message of the parable becomes crystal clear: anyone who determinedly resists sham and injustice, faces it, names it, and denounces it until right is achieved, is acting as God does, is God-like.

Yes, through her persistence the widow becomes a kind of Gandhi or Martin Luther King figure. Against all odds she will endure until justice is done and God will be present. So the parable, I suggest, is not about strategies to wear down a reluctant God with non-stop prayer or threatening black eyes, but it's about justice, about little people who are like God whenever they persistently seek, often against terrible odds, to have justice done and truth vindicated; whenever—to update the story—they hold self-serving politicians' feet to the fire, work to have children insured and free of violence, uncover the greed and corruption that siphons off money from the poor, improve education, and break down barriers that separate people.

I hope you can see why I cited this gospel and offered this homiletic commentary. It is pure Marge, whom I instinctively think of, not as the valiant woman of Ecclesiastes but as this just woman of the Gospel, one who had a disdain for shallowness, a thirst for justice, an interest in contemporary events, who listened to National Public Radio to the day she died, a highly intelligent woman who challenged people's thinking and the unjust judges of this world.

It was these prophet-like characteristics that led her in her search to embrace Catholicism as an adult. She was in fact received into the Church by my friend, your own Father Anderson. Now Catholic, yet still bearing deep wounds of hurt and loss from her past, Marge eventually journeyed to St. Mary's. To our delight and enrichment she stayed.

She stayed and she lectored, led the morning office, sang in the choir, reached out ecumenically, helped the addicted, choreographed the monthly birthday celebrations, wrote the monthly Martha/Mary newsletters, oversaw the jewelry table at the Attic sales, made caustic observations, and as a kind of background music to all this, routinely engaged in that mutual enjoyment—arguing with Joan Henderson.

Over the years, her ongoing spiritual journey led her even more deeply into the Sophia Prayer Group here at St. Mary's, to the invitations of Centering Prayer, the challenges of Zen, and the peaceful practices of Buddhism. The fact is, all her life Marge remained the woman of the gospel, the stubborn truth seeker, the incisive commentator on the foibles of society and Church, and the wonderfully eccentric lady who in her eighties bought a bright red Volkswagon and yet, at the same time, lived simply and close to nature: how she loved her house, her trees, her birds, her cats! A colorful woman. An honest woman. A just woman.

Over the years since I've been gone I haven't had a chance to talk much to Marge except we exchanged meaningful notes on Christmas cards and when, in recent times, it's been my sad and painful duty to return on occasions like this, Marge always made it a point to come over and give me a hug and make some heartfelt remark.

A year or so ago, I recall, she was seriously ill and close to death but, amazingly, she astounded everyone and bounced back. This time, however, she didn't and has gone off to join the rest of the Morning Group. It boggles the mind to think of Marge, Madeline Tibbitt, Eileen Connair, Kay Simone, and Joan Henderson all sitting at the same table at the Heavenly Banquet stuffing bulletins. I suspect that sooner or later, for the sake of peace, they will be given their own room.

Prophet, seeker, just lady, may you rest in peace.

$\mathcal{R}osemary$ Emerging

(LUKE 9:28B–36)

The "type" here is the spouse initially overshadowed by her partner in parish ministry but who emerges strong in her own right. The framing of this homily is the Trans-figuration story. Some of her journey will be repeated in the homily for her husband, Ralph.

I am, as you know, substituting for Fr. Ed who is away this week. In a way, I wish he were here with his customary understanding and gentleness. He knew Rosemary and Ralph but he knew them in their latter days. But I have known them from the beginning and that, I think, makes it harder and, I guess, makes me feel sorry for myself. There are so many memories of them—and others—that cling to these walls. So many old and dear friends have died so recently and been buried from here. Just these past weeks there were Ed Valich, Pat Picco, and young Michael Berestecky whom I used to pick up and play with and whom I taught. And there is Gerry DiSalvo waiting in the wings.

It gets harder, I tell you, because we priests get a small glimpse of what only parents can feel when they lose a child. Because for us, cel-ibacy is simply not the negative of not marrying and having children; it is rather the positive of being soulfully wedded to one's people who become, as time goes on, not members or parishioners but family, one's children in Christ and to lose one of them is very hurtful. To consistently lose so many is beyond words.

But enough of that. I remember the Imholtes beginnings here so well. Young Tommy Imholte had snuck over from Lincroft and, like the gospel brothers James and John who went and told Peter "we have found the Messiah," he went home and told his folks, not that he found the Messiah, but at least they ought to come and hear this guy. Well, I was young and in clover and had black hair way back then. Slowly then the clan appeared. They came, they saw, and they decided to stay.

Ralph approached me one day shortly after—right at that very door—saying he wanted badly to be a deacon. My reply was that I would consider it only if he came up with some special ministry because, as I told him, if the next pastor didn't happen to like deacons, he would wind up sitting in the pew as an ordained cleric twiddling his thumbs. This way, if he had some independent ministry, he would have something to fall back on.

"So what would you like to do," I asked. I remember so well how he paused a moment and then said, "Well, I've been happily married for twenty-five years. I'd like to teach others how to do it." Fine, and we agreed then and there that the parish would send him away to study marriage counseling. Which he did and, well, the rest is history as he blossomed into other related jobs and became a fixture, a staff member, a handy man, and a friend who always, as he does to this day, called me "boss." Some boss.

But even then, early on, I was curious, very curious, about something. Who *was* that woman, I thought to myself? The woman, I mean, that made him so happy for twenty-five years and, as it turned out, who would do so for thirty more years; a woman, a wife, a childhood sweetheart, as I was to discover, an Irish lass named Rosemary who was quite willing to be in the background, content to be overshadowed by the hardiness of her spouse.

I soon found out who she was, what she was, as I watched her over the years. I noticed her as she was cajoled into working with her husband and even to participate by speaking in front of Pre-Cana and groups of spouses. I remember how many times when we were working Pre-Cana together in the spiritual center and were awaiting our turn to speak. Rosemary would sidle up to me, gently touch me on the arm as she always did and whisper that she was scared to death. But she did it and did it often and gradually she found her voice and, after years of that, I would hear certain groups speaking, no longer about Ralph's wife but about Rosemary's husband.

But all that ministry was a sideline. Her family and her faith were inseparably bound as the foundation of all that she was. They were her identity, her rock, and her salvation. One was the other. It was her fundamental calling. So over the years she braved family problems and loss with fortitude and trust in God all while gathering friends and admirers. She was especially close to her prayer-discussion group, many of whom are here this morning, who met for years and years in spiritual and social gatherings and who for years and years made their annual retreat pilgrimage to Weston Priory and who brought back the fruits of their encounter with God to enrich this parish. These were the kind of priorities that guided Rosemary's life.

In the latter years, she began to have various physical troubles here and there. And then there was, of course, the great trauma of her husband's stroke. And she put on the back burner her own ailments and dedicated herself to the man she married fifty-seven years ago and made those words "for better for worse, richer or poorer, in sickness and health" so blazingly real. Lately, her anguish was deepened by the inevitable separation when Ralph went to the nursing home and rehab in Brick and she herself eventually followed elsewhere in Matawan. They had hoped, like a seasoned Romeo and Juliet, to be reunited there but that reunion will have to wait.

Rosemary, in her own way, was quite a noble woman who simply grew and grew. She is gone now but I deliberately and readily have placed her in the context of the gospel of the Transfiguration we read. That's because I picture Rosemary on Mt Tabor. Like Jesus, her face is no longer lined or ravaged, but shines like the sun. Her garments, nursing-home issue, are dazzling. Her tubes and medications have dissolved in light. Her sicknesses have burst into fireballs of splendor like the wounds of Jesus' body. She is talking coherently, briskly, intelligently, not with Moses and Elijah, but with her mom and dad and the child she lost and myriads of friends. And she is laughing that small delightful laugh she had. And then—and then—on her Mt. Tabor, there is also that voice. There is that validating voice: "This is my chosen daughter, listen to her."

She was always chosen. Chosen by God in her Minnesota baptism. chosen by Ralph as a faithful spouse, chosen by the Father to be a wonderful mother, chosen by the Son to come here and enrich us, chosen by the Spirit, beyond her wildest imaginings, to teach others; chosen, last but not least, by us to be reliable friend, loyal companion, and fellow pilgrim.

Well, Rosemary has prematurely gone through her Lent of 2004. She had enough of sorrow and pain. Her passion is over. She didn't need more penance, no more forty days. So she has gone to her Resurrection early and why not? Now, resplendent with the resplendent Christ, she has arrived, enjoying the fruits of a good and faithful servant.

Husband Ralph. Children: Whitey, Cathi, Mary Jo, Tom, Mark; grandchildren: this is your spouse, your mother, your grandmother. Folks, this is our friend and let me tell all of you—family and friends—as clearly as I can, she has been transfigured and she shines.

She shines.

Homily for a
Young Suicide

(LUKE 11:7–17)

As I look out over this congregation brought here by the common bond of the tragic death of someone we knew, I know that words are inadequate to temper our grief. Therefore, I shall try to make my words brief and address them to three groups of people. The first words concern John; the second concern John's friends and peers and classmates who are here to the great credit of your friendship and sympathy for his family—in great numbers; and the third concern all of us, but especially John's family. As for John, I presume that no one here is unaware that he took his own life. I think we ought to say that out loud so that we can hear it publicly and not just whisper this open secret among ourselves, and so that we can try to deal with it. But I want to share with you that often this deed, in the confused mind of a troubled person, is done out of love. A misguided and wrong-headed love, but love nevertheless.

The thinking of a person who is deeply troubled frequently goes like this: I am a burden. I'm hurting people. I'm in the way. I'm making a mess of things. I'm unhappy and making others unhappy. I worry those nearest to me. It would be kinder for everyone if I took the burden off their shoulders, if I weren't here, if I ceased to be. That's the understandable but backwards logic that often is at work in a person so troubled he or she doesn't see or think clearly. And that's at least good to know. It's at least good to know that, as painful as suicide is for us, at bottom there is the truth that it is often done out of love and concern for others. It's not good thinking, but bad thinking that nevertheless has its roots in charity, not malice.

And we ought to remember that about John. His tender love, as he understood it, did him in.

As for you young people here in such great numbers, John's friends and companions: for you John's death raises a question. It is this. What are you going to do about your friend's death? I mean, after the pain and the shock, after the anger—maybe at John himself, probably at God—after the hurt and tears, what are you going to do about your friend's death? It's easy to cry in his memory. What are you going to do with your life in his memory when your tears have dried?

I want to share with you a story an uncle of mine, dead himself many years now, told me because he had been there. It might suggest an answer. He told me the story of Puccini, the great Italian writer of such classic operas as *Madame Butterfly* and *La Boheme*. It seems when Puccini was fairly young he contracted cancer, and so he decided to spend his last days writing his final opera, *Turnadot*, which is one of his most polished pieces. When his friends and disciples would say to him, "You are ailing, take it easy and rest," he would always respond, "I'm going to do as much as I can on my great masterwork and it's up to you, my friends, to finish it if I don't." Well, Puccini died before the opera was completed. Now his friends had a choice. They could forever mourn their friend and return to life as usual—or they could build on his melody and complete what he started. They chose the latter. And so, in 1926 my uncle was there—at the famous La Scala Opera House in Milan, Italy—when Puccini's opera was played for the first time, conducted by the famed conductor Arturo Toscanini. And when it came to the part in the opera where the master had stopped because he died, Toscanini stopped everything, turned around with eyes welling up with tears, and said to the large audience, "This is where the master ends." And he wept. But then, after a few moments, he lifted up his head, smiled broadly, and said, "And this is where his friends began." And he finished the opera.

You see the point—and the point of the question I asked you: What are you going to do about John's death? What are you going to do about his unfinished masterpiece? Will it be, in a month or so, life as usual? Or can you build on his humor, his ability, his fun, his unrealized dreams? I would suggest that if there is any fitting response to the shock of your friend's death it is life, your life, a life that's lived better, a life lived more selflessly, a life that makes a difference, a life that is honest and decent, a life that makes beautiful music for John and for the Lord. Across the chasm of death you can make John live. The music doesn't have to stop here today and doesn't have to be buried with John. You have your choice.

Finally, to all of you, to all of us, but especially to John's family, in this sad moment I leave you with an image of hope, of perspective. Picture yourselves standing on a dock beside one of those great old-time sailing vessels. It's standing there, sails folded, waiting for the wind. Suddenly a breeze comes up. When the captain senses the breeze as a forerunner of the necessary wind, he quickly orders the sails to be let down and sure enough the wind comes, catches the sails full force, and carries the ship away from the dock where you are standing.

Inevitably you or someone on that dock is bound to say, "Well, there she goes!" And from our point of view it indeed does go. Soon the mighty ship, laden with its crew and goods, is on the horizon where water and sky meet and it looks like a speck before it disappears. It's still mighty and grand, still filled with life and goods, but it's left us. We're standing on the dock quite alone. But, on the other side of the ocean, people are standing in anticipation, and as that speck on the horizon becomes larger and larger they begin to cry something different. They are crying with joy, not abandonment, "Here she comes!" And at the landing there is welcome, joy, embracing, and celebration.

We miss John. He is quickly receding from our sight, and this funeral and his burial at the cemetery are our farewells, our versions of "There he goes." But goes where? From our sight, from our embrace, from our care and love and friendship. How we miss that, how we will miss him! But he is not diminished, nor made poorer. We must remember on faith that "Here he comes!" is the cry on the eternal shore where Jesus, who understands the human heart even when it goes wrong, is waiting. And there is John, now forever larger than life, filled with life, intoxicated with life and laughter and in the arms of the One who makes all things new again, the One who says, "Welcome, John. Welcome home."

Homily for a Mother

(MATTHEW 15:21–28)

Jesus left that place and went away to the district of Tyre and Sidon. Just then a Canaanite woman from that region came out and started shouting, "Have mercy on me, Lord Son of David; my daughter is tormented by a devil." But he did not answer her at all. And his disciples came and urged him, saying, "Send her away, for she keeps shouting after us." He answered, "I was sent only to the lost sheep of the house of Israel." But she came and knelt before him, saying, "Lord, help me." He answered, "It is not fair to take the children's food and throw it to the dogs." She snapped back, "Yes, Lord, yet even the dogs eat the crumbs that fall from their master's table." Knowing when he was defeated, Jesus answered her, "Woman, great is your faith! Let it be done for you as you wish." And her daughter was healed instantly.

And the woman smiled.

The word of the Lord. More or Less.

She's been a relatively short time dying, our mother, and the head has sensible things to say. She was, after all, ninety-one, a long time to live—and to live it in good physical and mental health almost to the last. Although growing progressively weak, she was never in pain. When we finally persuaded her to go to a doctor—it was her first visit in forty-seven years—the kindly doctor started to chide her, but he was no match for her repartee and wit and the patent fact that he was in his forties while his doctor-avoiding patient was in her nineties and he should be so lucky. So he surrendered and smiled and, like so many others, fell under her spell.

We never had, like some children, to bear the cross of years and years of disability and nurses and hospitals or nursing homes or hospice like so many others have. We bore all these things less than a year and that was hard enough, but we've been fortunate. As for her, outside of the great loss of her husband, Charles, and our Dad, she, unlike her peers, never had to bury any of her six children. Even in her final stage which lasted about nine or ten months—during which, I am compelled to say out of decency and gratitude, our brother Dick and especially our sister Rita, bore the brunt of her constant care and attention—she remained mentally alert and, at times, funny though she knew it was time (she was always savvy) and wanted to die. Meanwhile, she gave us time to tell her over and over again that we loved her and she us.

And there were other blessings. Two days before she died, my sister from Las Vegas having flown in, we celebrated Thanksgiving together even though the feast was a month away. I remember exactly the grace I was asked to give: "Almighty God, we thank you for this food and the hands that prepared it. And we thank you for our mother, her long life and her longer love. Amen." Two days later, as I said, she died. It was on November 4, the feast of St. Charles. We all know what happened. God said to Dad, "Charles, it's your feast day. What would you like more than anything else in the world?" He replied simply, "My wife." And God said, "So be it."

She was popular, beloved, highly intuitive, witty, forthright—*very* forthright, sharply so at times: you always knew where she stood—stylish and civic minded serving on PTA boards, treasurer to the Public Library, and carrying babies to foster homes for Catholic Charities. For an immigrant and baker's wife who knew what it was to work hard to carve out a life for herself and her family, she managed a good life, a good name, good children, a good home and, finally, a good death.

When people hear her age and her history, they say we were lucky to have her so long and that, well, after all she *was* ninety-one. They are right. We were lucky. It was time to go. And rather than see this in-charge woman, this strong woman lie helpless and dependent, which was galling to her, we were glad to see her go. The head nods in assent.

But, just when common sense and simple human experience have their say, just when the head prevails, the heart intrudes. The telltale, irrational heart which says that she was not just an unusual statistic with fabulous genes, but a wife, widow, sister—her remaining sister, who is ninety-six, Aunt Kate, is still alive and well and sharp—aunt, grandmother with ten grandchildren, great grandmother with thirteen great-grandchildren, mother-in-law, fast, steadfast friend, the hundred people who turned out for her ninetieth birthday last year, and the endless crowds at her wake giving testimony to that. In short, the heart knows of connections and relationships and the love and the hate, the virtues and the faults of this woman and we have all been deeply, irrevocably, touched by them all.

But, for us, she was the quintessential mother, fierce in her devotion, the kind they write gospels about, the kind that Rudyard Kipling wrote about:

> *If I were hanged on the highest hill,*
> *Mother o' mine, O mother o' mine !*
> *I know whose love would follow me still,*
> *Mother o' mine, mother o' mine !*
> *If I were drowned in the deepest sea,*
> *Mother o' mine, mother o' mine!*
> *I know whose tears would come down to me,*
> *Mother o' mine, mother o' mine!*
> *If I were damned by body and soul,*
> *I know whose prayers would make me whole,*
> *Mother o' mine! O mother o' mine!*

That was Mom. So, even though we know that we couldn't keep her forever, the length of her days actually made it harder to let go for she had become such a part of our emotional and spiritual landscape. So while the head dictates "get a hold of yourself," the heart weeps deeply and profoundly.

What helps is the one thing that mediates the head and the heart, and that is faith. She always had great faith. She was not naive and knew well enough human foibles in low and high places, in and out of the Church. She, like many another, was perplexed by all the rapid changes in society and in the Church, but she always knew that God had the last word and was in charge. She had a lively devotion to the Blessed Mother and had her rosary with her to the end and had no doubt that *that* mother would see *this* mother through.

Faith was a thread through all her life as it was our father's. For them faith was not a spectacular affair, just quiet devotion and fidelity, prayerfulness, everyday honesty and integrity, telling the truth, keeping one's promises, regular churchgoing and the unshakable belief that all was ultimately in God's hands.

It is this faith which had gathered us here in this church this morning which was, for sixty-seven years, a second home to her and to us all, where we were baptized, received First Communion, confirmed, married, buried, where I celebrated my first Mass, and which still is second home for our brother and sister and nephew who live in New Brunswick. It is this faith that says to the head, "Rejoice that you had her so long." It is this faith that says to the heart, "Rejoice that I have her now!"

And, having her now, God nods towards a large room and simply says, "You have some people waiting for you." The last sound is a mighty shout as she enters and closes the door behind her. And, after a pointed remark to long-time friend Kay Gleason about the decor, she sets about immediately preparing a place for her children.

That's the way she was, is and forever will be. Amen.

Homily for an Aunt

The framework here is the comparison of this Aunt Kate to television's Aunt Bee and therefore a reverent throwback to a more innocent age.

Today we have come to bury Aunt Kate. That very title says it all. She was a throwback to an age when family and neighborhood cohesion were facts and she was, and was known as, "Aunt Kate" to everyone. She was "Aunt Bee" long before the Andy Griffith show came along. No one called her Mrs. Nicorvo. Even casual aquaintances of every color and nationality, total strangers and, of course, family, called her Aunt Kate. She was one of those background people who form the context of comfort and security for children. She was a vital and taken-for-granted thread in the fabric of our lives. She was a presence. She was simply there, and when she was, we all felt reassured.

Every generation has its memories of this long-lived woman. Those of us who are older remember that each and every one of us was king and queen when we went to her house and stayed overnight. Breakfast in bed, favorite foods, and all the rest. We loved going to her house where we would play to a background punctuated with the refrain of an alarmed, "Richard!" and "Lillian!"

We delighted in her colorful neighbors like the Credicos. As a cashier, and with the connivance of John Zanzileri, she let us in for free to the movies. Why shouldn't we get the best seats with Louie and Albert as ushers? Oh yes, she was famous for her beef tea, paper-thin veal cutlets, and saucer-sized stuffed mushrooms.

Her home and heart were always open. Hospitality was as natural to her as breathing. She took care of her mother and our grandmother until she died. She took in our brother Jimmy to fatten him up. She was mother and eventually nurse to Mary Casey and grandmother to Corrine and Mary and Michael and Aunt to all the rest. She was, of course, sister to Uncles Joe, John and Angelo and Mary, Celesta and my mother, Colette, who had her own forthright views on Aunt Kate, as she did everything else.

I guess what I'm trying to say is that, as I said before, Aunt Kate is a throwback to an earlier age; a time when family meant everything and everyone's home was open to everyone else; when her favorite phone call was, "come over for a cup of coffee"; when every relative was a surrogate parent and you moved comfortably and unconsciously within an enveloping and protective framework of those who loved you. Aunt Kate represented all that and that's why her passing seems the passing of an era.

She lived longest of a long-lived family: five months short of a hundred years. Her last years, as you know, were spent in McCarrick Nursing home where my sister Rita and nephew John took constant loving and faithful care of her. For the most part she looked really great. Even several times when we thought it might be the end, she surprised us and sprung back.

Only near the end, say for the past six to nine months, did she begin occasionally to slip into the past. She would talk about being in a hotel in New York or Uncle Richard being home. But at ninety-nine she was entitled. Most times she would recognize us, but sometimes it would take a minute or two. Sometimes she would hold past and present together as the time I visited her and we had a very lucid conversation. As I left I wheeled her down to the elevator and said goodbye. And just as I got on, she said, "Oh, and send up Mrs. Credico. She's waiting for me." I said, "I'll tell her."

It was important that Aunt Kate should be in McCarrick nursing home, a Catholic nursing home. Like her family, she was very devout. Going to Mass every day was the high point of her life. In many respects, she didn't have an easy life but her faith kept her anchored.

She protested but was secretly flattered when Father Thul and Father Maurice, the chaplains, used to refer to her as "Saint Catherine." Maybe they weren't too far off.

It became obvious that in the past three weeks she was reaching some kind of critical stage. The good people at McCarrick would call Rita and alert her. So we went up to see her on Dick's birthday, November 17 and she was drowsy. We talked to her but didn't stay long as she lapsed into sleep. Another call the day before she died brought us again to visit her.

She was having trouble breathing. They had given her morphine to keep her pain-free. She was sedated and found it hard to stay awake but we talked to her even though she appeared to be out of it. Then, before we left, I said to her, "Would you like me to give you a blessing?" Then she suddenly looked at me and, quite focused, responded, "That would be nice."

Those were her last words. "That would be nice." The last of her clan, she died peacefully in her sleep on Thanksgiving morning. John got the call and called his mother and she called you—and here we are.

Somehow I picture the Good Lord saying to her, "Aunt Kate"— even *he* called her Aunt Kate—"Aunt Kate, would you like to spend Thanksgiving with your family? Would you like to see your parents and brothers and sisters? Would you like to see your children and Richard? Would you like to be with your friends?"

And Aunt Kate answering, "That would be nice."

And so it was done. It was nice. *She* was nice. May she rest in peace. Amen.

Homily for a Brother

This homily is included simply as a personal tribute to a beloved and gifted brother who died after a four-year struggle with pancreatic cancer.

As much as, like all of us, I had ample time to grasp and prepare for Jim's death, and as much as I thought that by this time I was emotionally depleted and cried out, I still find it painfully difficult to stand here today without fear of losing control. As Jim was near death, I told him of my weakness and misgivings and he suggested that I tape my words and have Father Brubaker lip-sync them. And we laughed together before we told each other, once more, how much we loved each other.

That wit and that declaration of love was Jim to the end. When people ask me what he was like I would always call up in my mind a favorite passage from Chaim Potok's celebrated novel, *The Chosen.* In a famous scene, the father is complaining in anguish to his friend Reuven about his precociously brilliant son Daniel, recalling how Daniel, at four years old, was able to read a tale in Yiddish about a poor Jew and his pitiable struggle to get to Israel before he died. And the boy, proud of himself, repeated the story back to his father from memory like he was reciting the phone book. And the father is smitten to the heart and cries out to God, "What have you done to me? A mind like this I need for a son? A heart I need for a son, a soul I need for a son. Compassion I want from my son, righteousness, mercy, strength to suffer and carry pain, that I want from my son, not a mind without a soul!"

I doubt if Jim's father—my father—ever prayed that, although he was a very prayerful man, or that he ever read *The Chosen*, although he read and spoke Yiddish fluently. But it is the most perfect reverse description of Jim Bausch that I know. He *was* a Daniel, very bright and intelligent, but, oh, he was a Daniel with heart, compassion, righteousness, mercy, and strength that carried suffering and pain, his own and others'. He was a mind with a very deep soul.

Yes, he *was* a Daniel. This blue-eyed child, this engaging, witty, intelligent man of open and generous heart, character, and integrity; this gourmet cook and raconteur whom I used to describe to my friends as a "Renaissance Man," so wide was his knowledge: from The Beach Boys to Beethoven, from Thomas Aquinas to Tommy Lasorda, from John Rockefeller, whom he knew, to John LeCarré, about whom he knew everything. What he didn't know was only an Internet click away. That is why it was the most natural thing in the world for him to be involved in the USF Academy of Lifelong Learning in Sarasota. On the home front we in the family called him "Dr. Jim," for every ailment we had, he had read something about it, quoted the research, and suggested the right medicine. Even though he was practicing without a license, he was our consultant in residence.

Jim was instinctively compassionate. He was the idealist who was among the first to join the Peace Corps, became CEO of Save the Children, worked at the Ford Foundation, and chaired other foundations. In short, Jim gave back abundantly to the community. He was genuinely generous and genetically moral. This Daniel with a laughing heart would show up and wash your floor, send you a helpful gadget, look up information that could aid you. He was uncannily sensitive to the needs of others. He remembered not only birthdays and anniversaries, but also the in-between things: when you were about to go to college, when exam time approached, when a marriage was troubled, when you needed money, when you were sick. About a half-dozen years ago I was rushed to the hospital for an emergency operation. When I awoke in the post-op room in Freehold, New Jersey, the first one I saw as I opened my eyes was my brother Jim from Siesta Key, Florida. He was like that. It's no small wonder that he asked that donations in his name be made to the Child Health Foundation in Maryland.

Jim was a presence, a brightness. He had personality when that word meant wit and sensitivity anchored to character. When I called him two days before he died, he could no longer speak, only grunt to acknowledge my comments. I called my brother Charlie afterward and told him that I didn't know how Jim could continue. He must have a strong heart, I commented. Charlie agreed and then added, "and a big heart." Indeed.

He also had faith. He was a religious person. In one of our many conversations, he told me how all his life he prayed every day. He made his peace with the church, went to Mass, was grateful for the kindly ministrations of his pastor and my classmate, Father Brubaker, received the sacraments, and gave himself over to God. In his last weeks his faith deepened profoundly and my last words to him were, "May God ease your passage." This Mass is his fervent wish. His ashes, to be scattered directly in front of this church, is his returned gift to God of a gifted life, a reminder to all who daily pass them by that a righteous person is there.

He was a long time dying. About four years ago, as you know, the possibility and then the actuality of cancer began to surface, and about two years ago it metastasized into one of the worst kind, fourth-level pancreatic cancer. Few live beyond four or five months. But Jim did and confounded everybody. With great support from his wife, Janet, and a group of truly extraordinary doctors who dispensed medicine, compassion, and hugs in equal amounts, he faced every challenge. And, for a long time, he succeeded. Jim in fact became the Poster Boy among the medical community for surviving so long, even appearing in the university newsletter. Again, you usually don't last long with that kind of cancer.

Last year his amazed doctor told him that he shouldn't be there in his office talking. Jim replied that three things kept him alive: good genes, lots of prayer, and determination. And determination he had, as he took on every new experimental procedure and medication. He was supposed to die in 2002, for sure in 2004. He made it to 2006. Characteristically this ever-sensitive man did not want to die on a holiday. Janet's mother died on Mother's Day and he didn't want to repeat that kind of an association. Stunningly, he did avoid the holidays for his departure. In 2005 he was delighted that he made Thanksgiving and then Christmas and Chanukah. He made New Year's and even, unexpectedly, his seventieth birthday on May 1. He wrote, "I didn't think I'd see last Christmas, Chanukah, or the New Year. Now, to everyone's surprise, I am about to fulfill the biblical lifespan of three score and ten years, a birthday I had no realistic hope of celebrating."

But if that long-time dying, especially these last few months, was a hardship, especially to Janet and his family, at the same time it was also a gift in more ways than one. It gave us all, family and friends, a chance to say many times how much we loved one another; to reminisce, to laugh and cry, to draw closer together. Not all families and friends get that chance.

I said Jim was an idealist, a world-fixer. There is a phrase that comes out of the mystic tradition in Judaism, the Kabbalah, called *tikkun olam*. It translates into something like "fixing up the world." It rests on the assumption that the world is imperfect, even that God intentionally left it imperfect, because he had created human beings to become God's agents in making creation proper. Moreover, the Master of the Universe, knowing human beings couldn't do it alone, insisted they must join up with others, look for friends, companions.

Jim was, as I said, a world-fixer and he had a talent for finding such world-fixing companions, for making fast and lifelong friends. His friendships from St. Peter's College, as you heard so ably, are legendary: John Fanning, Frank Mertz, Dick Keating, Dick Jeanneret, Harry Vitting—an awesome sextet by any standards—presided over by the late eccentric, Father Murphy, S.J. His friends from the places he worked, the Academy of Lifelong Learning, neighbors, his doctors, are many; and there are special friends such as Barry Gaberman, Joe Manhurter, Marilyn Harwell, Sid Landau, Bill Hooker, Lois Selden, Steve Schlossberg, and others too numerous to mention. That you are all here, from every background, tradition, and way of life is testimony to our common humanity and compassion that transcend all the boundaries human beings can invent. You are the folk who accompanied him while he was fixing up the world and now you accompany us and, on behalf of the family, I thank you deeply and sincerely.

Finally, even with all of his family and friends and remarkable endurance, time ran out as it had to. At the beginning of June he and his doctors decided to end all further procedures. He gave himself over to God and to the lovely ministrations of hospice. If, as I said, the gifted time we did have enabled us to say what we should have, it also gave Jim a time to plan. Jim was, if nothing else, a planner, a researcher. He liked to have things all spelled out, a characteristic I share. He wrote e-mails and letters, took care of all legalities, and, much to my minor dismay, even planned every aspect of this funeral. Mildly exasperated at one point, I complained to him that while he was at it, why didn't he write this homily. Like Jack Benny, when confronted by a thug snarling, "Your money or your life!" there was a pause: "I'm thinking! I'm thinking!" he said. We laughed.

He put me very much in mind of the American writer E.B. White, best known as the author of the children's classic, *Charlotte's Web*. In a moving piece that was written late in his life, he mused about his wife's gardening:

> As the years went by and age overtook her, there was something comical yet touching in her bedraggled appearance on this awesome occasion...the small hunched-over figure, her studied absorption in the implausible notion that there would be yet another spring, oblivious to the ending of her own days, which she knew perfectly well was near at hand, sitting there with her detailed chart under those dark skies in the dying October, calmly plotting the resurrection.

That was Jim. That was my brother, calmly plotting his resurrection.

Yes, he was my brother, but beyond that, he was, first and foremost, profoundly and endearingly, Janet's husband—she was his sun, moon, and stars—and he was Jennifer and David's precious father,

Rachel's grandfather, nieces' and nephews' uncle, godchildren's god-father, and dearest friends' dearest friend. His was a good life. His was a good death.

Jim agreed. He could write near the end:

> Janet and I have been looking back over these past years and it is clear that while others might live longer than I seem destined to, no one could have had it better than we. It has been a wonderful life together, blessed with Jennifer and David, being part of two terrific families, having marvelous-ly supportive friends, and reflecting with joy and gratitude on some accomplishments and experiences we have had. I wouldn't trade my life for anyone else's, nor would Janet, which says a lot.

And among his last words were these: "Dying is a part of life. I'm ready, and I surely have nothing to complain about. I'm still the luck-iest, most blessed person I know."

That is, outside of us who were privileged to know him.

Part Three

Appendices

Instructions for My Funeral

PRE-PLANNING PAPERS

Believers, like many others, put off thinking about death. A funeral is often handled in a rush and in a manner that does not reflect the wishes of the deceased (because survivors often don't know them). The following directives have been distributed in some parishes to enable Christians to have some say in their own funerals and over their own bodies. Far from being morbid, this approach is both a courtesy and a responsibility. You are invited to fill out these forms and request the parish, mortuary, and the relatives to keep them on file.

INFORMATION FOR THE CHURCH

Funeral instructions for _____
(Name)

To assist those responsible for my funeral arrangements, I wish the following:

1. At my death I want _____ to be contacted.
(Mortuary)

2. I (have/have not) consulted with the funeral director of the above named mortuary regarding the following

   ❑ Selection of (casket/vault)

   ❑ Selection of cemetery (plot/crypt)

   Other specific directions not covered above: _____

   _____

3. I wish the following:

   ❑ Morning Mass and burial

   ❑ Evening Mass and burial

   ❑ Evening Rosary with morning Mass and burial

   ❑ Evening Prayer or wake service with morning Mass and burial

   ❑ Graveside service only

   ❑ Memorial service

   ❑ Other: _____

4. I want these services conducted at:

   ❑ Church

   ❑ The funeral home

   ❑ Other: _____

5. I wish the following person to conduct my funeral service:

1st choice: _____

2nd choice: _____

6. I wish the following person to give my eulogy:

1st choice: _____

2nd choice: _____

7. I (do/do not) wish to have an open casket.
Other specific directions not covered above: _____

_____

8. I would prefer, that instead of sending flowers, my friends make memorial gifts to: _____

9. I make the following suggestions of materials that I would like to have used in my service: _____

_____

10. Scripture passages to be read: _____

_____

11. Prayers: _____

12. Music: _____

Other: _____

INSTRUCTIONS TO MORTUARY

$\overline{\qquad\qquad\qquad}$
(Date)

1. My Name: _____

2. Address: _____

3. Date of birth: _____ Place of birth: _____

4. Citizen of _____
   (Country)

5. ❑ Single   ❑ Married   ❑ Widowed   ❑ Divorced

6. Name of Spouse: _____

7. Last occupation: _____ How long? _____

8. Kind of business: _____

9. Last Employing Co. or Firm: _____

10. Social Security No. _____

11. *If Veteran:* Rank & Branch of Service: _____

    Name of War: _____

    Date & Place Entered Service & Discharge: _____

    Service No. _____

    I would want an American Flag for my family   ❑ yes   ❑ no

Final Disposition: ❑ Burial   ❑ Cremation   ❑ Donation

A. I leave this to my next of kin: _____

B. I have made arrangements regarding my cremated remains or interment as follows: _____

_____

C. Designate location of burial plot, cemetery, mausoleum, columbarium, or other instructions: _____

_____

D. This authorizes release of my remains to: _____
(name mortuary)

_____   _____
        (Witness)   *(Signature)*

INFORMATION FOR SURVIVORS

1. Key person to be notified: _____

   Phone number: _____

2. Church: _____

   Phone number: _____

3. Doctor: _____

   Phone number: _____

4. Funeral Home: _____

   Phone number: _____

5. Executor of will: _____

   Phone number: _____

Relatives and friends to be notified: _____

_____

_____

Insurance Policies

Company	Policy No.	Agent

VETERANS RECORDS

Identification Number: _____

VA Office to Notify: _____

Location of discharge papers: _____

Location of Will: _____

Location of Safe Deposit Box: _____

Attorney names, address, phone number

_____

_____

_____

Bank Accounts: Name of bank, type of account (Stocks & Bonds)

_____

_____

_____

Outstanding Loans and Credit Obligations

_____

_____

_____

BIOGRAPHICAL INFORMATION

Date baptized: _____

Location of baptismal papers: _____

Confirmation papers: _____

For Married Persons: Place and date of marriage: _____

_____

Pursuant to the Uniform Anatomical Gift Act, I hereby give, effective upon my death:

A. _____ Any needed organ or parts

B. _____ Parts of organs listed _____

_____

_____   _____
           Signature   *Date*

Witnessed by: _____

Witnessed by: _____

TO WHOM IT MAY CONCERN

This letter is not a request—it is an order. I have tried to live with dignity and I want to die the same way. If my fate is such that I should become old and afflicted with an irrevocable illness and unable to make a rational decision, you are hereby instructed to give the physician orders that he/she must not attempt to prolong my life by using extraordinary means; by which I mean:

1. _____   2. _____

3. _____   4. _____

I have made this decision so as to relieve you of the responsibility of making it.

With appreciation and love,

_____   _____
Signature   *Date*

Witnessed by: _____

The Mystery of Death

This is a follow-up section to the funeral homilies. These homilies attempt to deal with the ancient (and insoluble) theodicy problem: how can a good God permit such evil as we see every day in our world? This theoretical problem becomes quite real for certain people at the time of a death in the family. I know one lady who left the church after her twenty-two-year-old son was killed in an automobile accident. She demanded to know why she, a good churchgoer, didn't deserve better than that. God either didn't care or was impotent.

The questions are angry and heartbreaking. We've all heard (felt?) them: Where was God when my son/daughter/spouse/parent died? Why didn't God cure him or her when we all prayed so hard? How can I ever trust God again? How can I return to church?

Recoiling from any insensitive comments that it was "God's will" or "your faith was not strong enough" I have no more answers than others. I can only offer approaches that circle the problem for those grieving and questioning. These four homilies, scattered throughout the liturgical year, are brought together here in the hope of providing some context when painful questions arise.

Love Trusts

MATTHEW 11:25–30

Some time ago, twenty-three-year-old Patrick Purdy killed five small children in a schoolyard. And then he turned the gun on himself and took his own life. So I ask you to imagine, however difficult it is because it's so uncomfortable, I ask you to imagine that you are the parent of one of those slain children. You run down the litany of the feelings you absolutely have to have gotten: total shock and disbelief; grief and horror; and then, of course, finally rage.

But if that weren't bad enough, there is one more pain, which is probably the worst of all, and that is you can't even vent your rage on anyone because the young man was irresponsible; he was psychotic; but worse than that, he is dead.

So you think of that. There's no place to put your anger, no place to release your hate. There's nobody's chest that you can pound; there's not even an idiot face that you can yell at. There's no human being left that you can curse. There's no one around that you can even prosecute or that you can imprison. It's extremely unfair, to say the least. There's just raw frustration, with no place to go; except you can go inward and poison your system, and that can deteriorate your health. And, of course, there's always the third outlet: God.

I thought of this when I heard Friday of the death of Bill Johnson, who was jogging along in good health at Brookdale College where he was the athletic director. And not only did he just drop dead, but it was a year ago that his own young son died of a brain tumor. And so you listen to things like that, and read stories of five innocent children slain playing in their schoolyard, and then you ask, if not out loud, How do you square that with God?

And I think the question gets extremely poignant when you add, How do you square these things with God, especially when you have been good, and you have kept the commandments; and feel, rightly so, that after all, you deserve some consideration? You can't help but think that a God who does not come across for the faithful ones is either pretty fickle or pretty powerless. Now that's understandable.

In the light of St. Paul's epistle (1 Corinthians 13), these incidents force us to the deep question, the question that you and I don't like to look at because, again, it's not a terribly comfortable question; and it's very challenging, and goes right to the heart of the matter. Beneath all these tragedies and anger, and rage and perplexity, is the question that sooner or later we have to try to wrestle with: What is your relationship with God?

And the only way to respond to that is to say, "Well, what is my relationship with other people?" Fundamentally, we all have to say that my relationship with other people has to at least try to rest on some kind of a trust, even in perplexing and strained times; and maybe *especially* in perplexing and strained times. We accept, without question, that our relationships with other human beings are not a "tit for tat" contract type of thing: "I will be loyal and so will you. I will be honest and so will you. I will be faithful and so will you. I will do everything I should and so will you." It just doesn't happen that neatly, does it? It just doesn't happen that way.

And because it doesn't, and because we know that relationships are imperfect and are not based on guarantees but on trust, we make considerable room for forgiveness and reconciliation, for change and growth; for uncertainty; for hope; and, ultimately, as St. Paul says, for love, a love that somehow will overcome all the deficiencies. But when it comes to our relationship with God, we change the rules, don't we? You think about that. We come up with this extremely odd "contract" notion. "God, I kept all the commandments, so how could you let my daughter get sick? How could you let my marriage fail, and disintegrate and break up? How could you let my innocent child get machine-gunned at school? *How could you!*"

It always amazes me when Christians say things like that, although I can understand it when they're under stress. For after all, Christians every single year celebrate a two-thousand-year-old story of a man who was faithful to God, who kept all the commandments, and who wound up being spit upon, and stripped, and scourged, and crowned with thorns, and hung on a cross to die; and this was one about whom God said, "This is my beloved son."

But anyway, what gets exposed here is the one-dimensional shallowness of our relationship with God, which we would not tolerate with other people. When we analyze it, our relationship with God is one of contract, not of trust. With God, somehow, we want not trust, but guarantee; not acceptance, but explanation; not faith, but certainty; not adventure, but predictability; not ambiguity, but a flow chart; not mystery, but a signed contract. Is that the way you treat other people in your life? Why do we do it with God?

Or are we ready to trust that God, being God, will have the last word in all the madness and absurdities of life, as God did in the absurdity and madness of what happened to God's beloved son? And even there, what's our view of Jesus? I have a feeling that for most of us it's a distorted view: Jesus is the great detached one, who up his sleeve had the master plan laid out, and he says, "Well, I can put up with a little bit of fuss because in the end we're all going to live happily ever after." But the fact is that Jesus was not the great detached one. If anything, Jesus comes across in Scripture as the great pilgrim, the authentic life who did not escape the human condition; who did not know the master plan; who did not have the completed script; who took life day by day and let life's evil have its full play, while his Father, who would not remove human freedom with all its potential for good and evil, wept at what happened to him.

And in the end, the Father dried his tears and raised Jesus up, as Jesus trusted that he would, although he had his last-minute doubts: "My God, my God, why have you forsaken me?" That's faith. Faith is belief surrounded by doubt, with doubt getting stronger in troubled times. But that's relationship. Just like husbands and wives, and brothers and sisters, and friends and lovers; with all the unfairness of life, you have to trust—or you die.

Let me share with you the true story of a soldier named Joseph Schultz. Just over one hundred years ago Adolph Hitler was born. In his fifty-six years on the planet he did incredible harm and was responsible for millions of terrible deaths. Yet in all of the horror that he unleashed, there are pinpoints of light and nobility. And this German soldier, Joseph Schultz, who was the same age as Patrick Purdy, who machine-gunned children in the schoolyard, was one of these pinpoints.

He was sent to Yugoslavia shortly after the invasion. He was a loyal, young German soldier on patrol, and one day the sergeant called out eight names, his among them. They thought they were going on a routine patrol, and as they hitched up their rifles, they came over a hill, still not knowing what their mission was. There were eight Yugoslavians there, standing on the brow of the hill; five men and three women. It was only when they got about fifty feet away from them, when any marksman could shoot out an eye of a pheasant, that the soldiers realized what their mission was.

The eight soldiers were lined up. The sergeant barked out, "Ready!" and they lifted up their rifles. "Aim," and they got their sights. And suddenly in the silence that prevailed, there was a thud of a rifle butt against the ground. The sergeant, and the seven other soldiers, and those eight Yugoslavians stopped and looked. And Private Joseph Schultz walked toward the Yugoslavians. His sergeant called after him and ordered him to come back, but he pretended not to hear him.

Instead, he walked the fifty feet to the mound of the hill, and he joined hands with the eight Yugoslavians. There was a moment of silence, then the sergeant yelled, "Fire!" And Private Joseph Schultz died, mingling his blood with those innocent men and women. What was found on his body was an excerpt from today's reading from St. Paul. The excerpt was: "Love does not delight in evil, but rejoices in the truth. It always protects, always trusts, always hopes, and always perseveres."

Private Joseph Schultz was drawn into a war that was absurd. He was drawn into an event that was evil that he did not understand. He was drawn into a perplexity and an unfairness of life, and he wondered what God could possibly have in mind. And yet he trusted that his sacrifice would make a difference, and that God would be faithful.

He had no guarantee. He had no special insight into any master plan. He had no assuredness, he only had a relationship with God, whom he trusted, even when he did not understand God. And I think that is what Paul is saying.

There is hardly anyone hearing this who cannot say that life has been unfair. Many of you are in a broken relationship; some of your children have bitterly disappointed you; others among you are dying of cancer. And you say, "Life is unfair," and you're right. And you say, "I've been faithful. I go to church every Sunday and I follow all the rules. How could God do this to me? I've lost a relationship. I've lost a son. I've lost a spouse. I've lost a parent. I've lost a job. I've lost health. Is this the way God treats God's beloved ones?"

And all that I ask you to do as you get angry with God, is, for heaven's sake, look at the crucifix. This is his beloved son. In the crucifix is the message that you trust the relationship, as Jesus had to. It is permissible to get angry, and it is permissible to doubt, as Jesus did on the cross. But in the end you have to ask, What is your relationship with God? If it's a relationship of a contract, you have a right to abandon God and say, "You didn't keep your part of the bargain, and I'm not keeping mine. Goodbye. I've had it!"

But if it's a relationship, like with somebody you love, then you have to trust God. With people you love, even though you don't understand what they're doing and why they're doing it, or why they're acting that way, you stick with them, even when they're mentally and emotionally and physically ill. You hang in there even when you see no end and no light at the end of the tunnel. God asks for nothing less than that. God is friend, is beloved, is in relationship with you, and as in any relationship, God asks for your trust. The resurrection of Jesus Christ, who had his doubts, is proof that God will have the last word. So St. Paul is right, and Private Schultz is right, and Jesus is right. If God is love, love does not delight in evil, but love rejoices in the truth. Love always protects; love always trusts; love always hopes. And love always perseveres.

When the Miracles Stop

(JOHN 6:1–15,
17TH SUNDAY IN ORDINARY TIME,
CYCLE B)

"Jesus went across the sea of Galilee. A large crowd followed him because they saw the miracles he was performing..."

It's vacation time. It's summer time when the livin' is easy. Should I try to tease your minds and hearts in such a context? Should I offer something challenging that this gospel provokes? Well, why not? You can always complain to the pastor.

It's those opening words of the gospel I just cited that raise the issue. "A large crowd followed Jesus because they saw the miracles...." Well, I ask, who wouldn't follow? You'd be dense not to. My challenging question is, What happens when the miracles cease? When they dry up? Will we follow Jesus when there are no more miracles? Will I follow when my child is born genetically defective and all the prayers in the world aren't pulling in the miracle that would make her any different than a prospect for lifelong care? When my spouse is killed in an automobile accident and there is no miracle of resurrection, when I am diagnosed with a terminal illness and no miraculous cure appears? When bad things happen to good people and there are no miracles to right the equation? When, in a word, there are no miracles and no more God, at least none that I can detect, when faith is shaken if not evaporated altogether. Will we follow then? So again, my question: Will we follow Jesus when we no longer see miracles?

A woman who lost her child at birth, and almost her faith, writes:

> All my multilayered, carefully constructed faith was stripped away as I focused on one thing: the injustice that our little girl didn't have a chance to take even a single breath....[Even] prayer seemed so futile, even unnecessary, like throwing a glass of water on a burning house. I had prayed my entire pregnancy for the baby to be healthy—and she was. Carly was perfect but she wasn't alive, cooing in my arms. How could I not feel betrayed?...
>
> In the weeks following Carly's death, well-meaning friends and relatives called and sent hundreds of cards and letters offering helpless words of condolence. Most of their efforts said the same thing: "It was God's will. We cannot understand God's will." Those words kept me up at night for months, spinning through my frantic mind, tying me in philosophical knots. I know they were trying to help, but every time the issue of God's will sprang up, I was miserable. It got to the point where I couldn't even numbly smile or nod any more when the phrase inevitably popped up. I just clenched my teeth to keep from saying something I'd regret.

Finally, exhausted, this woman who lost her child and almost her faith, punctuates her long sorrow with these plaintive words: "Some may wonder why, after our experience, I still want to make the painful effort to believe. I can only respond that, despite my doubts, having seen the breathtaking perfection of my daughter's peaceful face, it is impossible to think God was not there." Somehow, beyond the miracle that never came, she sensed Someone.

Let's hold that in mind while I move to a short story I once read about a doubt-ridden Jesuit priest. Since age ten, he has been plagued by doubts. Finally, however, he develops a doubt that will not pass; he begins to doubt the love of God. In the face of his doubt, he prays for faith, but none comes. So, he prays for hope, but when that is not given either, he simply goes on with his duties: teaching, preaching, saying Mass. Then, one bright, clear day, after saying Mass, he is driving home to the rectory when he comes across a terrible automobile accident. A young man lies dying, trapped in an overturned car. The priest is able to force open the crumpled car door and manages to cradle the dying man in his arms.

Taking a vial of holy oil from his pocket, the priest anoints the dying man, pronouncing, "I absolve you from all your sins. In the name of the Father and of the Son and of the Holy Ghost. Amen." But, then, *nothing happens.* There is no shift in the world, no change in the dire situation, no word from heaven, not even any human rescuers come. Only the silent world and the dying young man's harsh, half-choked breathing. The priest begins to pray recited prayers, rote prayers, prayers about Mary, prayers to the Father in heaven. He feels foolish, but what else can he do, what else can he say? He wants that miracle.

He wonders, What would God do at such a moment, if there were a God? "Well, do it!" he says aloud, and hears the fury in his voice. "Say something!" But there was silence from heaven....What could anyone say to this crushed, dying thing, he wondered. What would God say if he cared as much as I?...The priest could see death beginning across the face of the young man, who suddenly turned in some dying reflex, his head tilted in the priest's arms, trusting, like a lover. And at once the priest, faithless, unrepentant, gives up altogether and bends over him and whispers, fierce and burning, "*I* love you," and continues until there is no breath, "*I* love you, *I* love you, *I* love you." A cry that meant that even if God didn't come through with a miracle, *he* loved the dying young man. What now?

This is hard, but I suggest in this story that the priest is fundamentally a converted man, even though he doesn't know it. He is a man who has quite painfully moved from a childish faith to a mature and hopeful one.

What happened is that the priest, when you come right down to it, was forced to give up his immature idea of a God who comes with miracle in hand when we whistle to make everything all right, in favor of a God who summons the faithful to be present when a need arises, to be God's incarnate divine mercy at this time and place. In other words, the priest, lacking a miracle, *himself* becomes the miracle. God was there and held that dying man through his arms.

So today's gospel in its own way poses the question: Will we follow Jesus when the miracles stop? When our daughter dies, when our son is killed? Will we, like the woman who lost her child, see the absent miracles as an invitation to seek the miracle-worker himself? Will we consider the possibility that, when all is said and done, after the shock is over and the tears are dried, *we* ourselves might be the miracle?

I don't know. It's tough to stand in someone else's shoes. I just know that, of course, the folks in the gospel story were sensible and savvy to follow Jesus *because* of the miracles he was performing, but I also know that folks are even more sensible and spiritually savvy to realize that the magic tricks are just that: tricks to get you to the magician and to be discarded once you have found him. We are challenged to learn to love Jesus for who he is rather than for the free bread he can give us. I think that dried-up miracles can help us focus on the real miracle, that *we* are called to be the compassion and presence of God. It is, as I said, a tough call, but a call nevertheless.

Anyway, it's something to think about on a summer day. As you heard, the gospel story had a happy ending. Lots of people saw miracles and were fed with a new one. But it's also time to think about those who saw none and are left excruciatingly hungry. Hungry for some answers, some sign, some way, ultimately, to live without miracles and still live with Jesus.

John the Baptist and Second Thoughts

(SECOND SUNDAY OF ADVENT, YEAR A, MATTHEW 3:1–12)

John the Baptist is the dominant figure in today's liturgy. He's a re-markable man in many ways. We know that he received a call from God. And he answered it. As a result, Matthew's gospel which we just heard starts off:

> When John the Baptizer made his appearance as a preacher in the desert of Judea, this was his theme: "Reform your lives! The reign of God is at hand." Then turning to the Pharisees and the Sadducees, he shouts, "You brood of vi-pers! Who told you to flee from the wrath to come? Give some evidence that you mean to reform....Every tree that is not fruitful will be cut down and thrown into the fire."

This obviously is not a man unsure of himself. On the contrary, this is a man on fire with purpose. This is God's prophet aiming for the jugular. A strong, confident man. He was called. He reacted without hesitation and began his mission. A straight man on a straight line.

But somewhere along the way—we don't know when—doubt be-gan to creep in. Was he right? Was he called by God or was all this self-delusion, all his fervent preaching for naught? *Was* cousin Jesus the one he was paving the way for? He wasn't so sure anymore.

Maybe after so many years, he was at a low point. Things weren't working out well. After all, at this time, he was no longer found along the Jordan but languishing in jail, detained in Herod's fortress of Machaerus, situated on the lonely desert heights overlooking the Dead Sea, awaiting who knows what! Or, as Matthew writes sparingly a few chapters later, "John was in prison." He had time to think. Maybe he had been all wrong, chosen the wrong path, bet on the wrong Messiah. Doubts made for troubled dreams. He decided to act.

Matthew gives us the account: "John in prison...sent a message through his disciples to ask him, 'Are you he who is to come or do we look for another?'" There it was. Plain, simple, and direct. "Just like John," Jesus thought to himself. Out loud, Jesus answered the delegation the best way he could: "Go and tell John what you have seen and heard: the blind receive their sight, the lame walk. The lepers are cleansed, the deaf hear, and the dead are raised, the poor have the gospel preached to them." And then he pointedly added with softness and compassion, "And blessed is anyone who takes no offense in me." He looked long at the departing disciples of John and then, when they were out of sight, commented, "I tell you, among those born of women no one is greater than John...."

John of Advent is many people throughout the ages. He is the initial *yea-sayer with second thoughts.* I have been faithful to God. I have kept trust. I have prayed. I have been active in ministry. I read all the right books, faithfully go to Mass, give to the poor. And things have not turned out all right. I recently received letters from two John the Baptist-type people. One woman is filling me in on her family. The boys are doing fine. But the girls. One is living with a man and is planning to marry him outside the church. The other married a Jewish man, had the children baptized Catholic, and now is converting to Judaism and is going to raise the kids—her grandchildren—Jewish. Another's daughter just has a baby six months ago. The doctors recently removed a tumor the size of a grapefruit from her daughter, who is very sick now with chemotherapy. The baby was born with a hole in her heart and a thumb that is dangling and has to be removed.

"Are you the one who is to come or shall we wait for another?" Throughout the ages how many have wondered this in their grief or bitterness or disappointment? Have I been wrong to be so faithful? Worse, have I been a fool? People prayed for my son, we had a prayer chain going, we believe in healing, pleaded for a miracle. He died anyway. Some whispered that it was because I didn't have enough faith. If I had only believed more firmly!

To come to terms with this quandary, especially for those of a charismatic spirituality bent, I invite you to listen to the words of a fine and insightful Southern Baptist minister named Al Staggs:

> My wife died in April of this year following a twelve-year battle with cancer, a particularly malignant melanoma. [Comments from well meaning-but-misguided friends about the healing power of faith] have compelled me once again to rethink my theology of healing. I confess that I have extremely low tolerance for the so-called faith healers or for the peddlers of healing. I'm aghast that anyone would dare to claim to understand the mind of God about any particular person or any particular illness.
>
> What these folks do to people is to hold out hope for a complete reversal of a person's physical condition. When the miracle does not occur, the lack of miraculous action can be attributed to a person's lack of faith, which only compounds the person's problems. Not only are these people terminally ill, but they are also being taught that they are not good Christians. In my weaker moments I am reminded of the passage from Matthew 7:22–23, where Jesus says, "Many will say to me on that day, 'Lord, Lord, did we not prophesy in your name, and in your name drive out demons and perform miracles?' Then I will tell them plainly, 'I never knew you. Away from me, you evildoers!'"
>
> A few weeks prior to my wife's death, visiting friends recounted story after story of "miraculous" answers to their prayers. After hearing a steady diet of incidents in which people were healed of their infirmities or found better-paying jobs, my wife looked over at both of them and said simply, "It hasn't worked that way for us."

Sometimes I just want to ask these people who become so excited about miraculous healing, "Has your vaunted prayer program yet kept anyone alive forever?" Eventually we all die, including those who were healed of their particular disease. No one has yet managed to avoid the grim reaper. So why save our success stories for just those precious few who have been allowed a few months or years longer than they would otherwise have had? There needs to be a major emphasis on God's grace and sufficiency for every illness and every situation. The Christian community should talk just as loud and long about God's Essence in the most hopeless situations as we do about the "miraculous healings."

[Henri] Nouwen had this to say about death: "Death does not have to be our final failure, our final defeat in the struggle of life, our unavoidable fate. If our deepest human desire is indeed to give ourselves to others, then we can make our death into a final gift. It is so wonderful to see how fruitful death is when it is a free gift."

Nouwen's words and his own approach to his life and to his recent death are a counterbalance against those whose "healing" hit-and-run ministries suggest that death is a defeat and that only miraculous cure is a victory.

Stories of miraculous healing have their place. The miracle of a believer's faith, however, in the face of terminal illness, and the faith of a loving family, is just as important as any story of a miraculous cure of an illness. Very few people experience a total reversal of illness. Most people diagnosed with terminal illness struggle through it to the very end. So let us hear the stories of the miraculous presence of God in the lives of these saints who are faithful to the end.

There is our key: holding onto the faithful presence of God in our worst moments, clinging to belief in the ultimate victory of his love which "will make all things new again." Look, no one is free of second thoughts, especially in times of crisis. Not even John the Baptist. Not even Jesus: "Father, if it is possible remove this cup from me." "My God, my God, why have you forsaken me!" But there is the response and life lesson: "Nevertheless, not my will but thine be done....Into your hands I commend my spirit—my gift."

In other words, as Staggs said, be assured of, and hold on to, the miraculous presence of God in times of seeming abandonment, in times when we are tempted to look for another. It's like the distraught woman who cried to the priest, "Where was God when my son died?" And he answered softly, "The same place when *his* Son died."

If John was one who received the call, reacted with certainty, and then lapsed into doubt, he is legion. But he gave his life for truth and God was in his fidelity, despite his doubt. Truly, no greater man was born of a woman.

And so too for us. Yes, pray for the miracle, the sudden cure. It happens. But also pray to discern that Divine Presence in the rhythmic pain, suffering, and death, and offer them as a gift, a gift that will be forever accepted by a love that never falters in a place where there are no more tears.

The
Divine Absence

(ISAIAH 42:1–4, 6–7, CYCLE A)

"A bruised reed he shall not break and a smoldering wick he shall not quench."

There is a scene in the play called *Ma Rainey's Black Bottom* written by the African American playwright, August Wilson. It's about some African American jazz musicians who are rehearsing in a Chicago recording studio. At some point they take a break from their rehearsal and begin to tell stories. One of them tells the story about a cousin of his, a minister whose sister in Atlanta was desperately ill and so he took a train to visit her. The train stopped in a little Georgia town to take on water and the minister got off the train to use the bathroom. He went into the station and was told, "Colored people can't use the bathroom in here; you have to use the outhouse."

So he went to the outhouse and while he was there the train left the station. There's the minister standing on a south Georgia platform—no train, no friends. Across the tracks there's a group of hostile young white men, and not wanting trouble, the minister simply starts walking up the railroad track. The group of men follow him. They surround him. They demand to know who he is and what he's doing. He tells them, "I am a minister." He shows them his Bible, he shows them his cross, he tells them his sister in Atlanta is sick and he's been left by the train. No matter. "Dance for us," they say.

"Dance! Why don't you dance for us?" Someone pulls out a pistol and begins to fire at the ground and they make him dance.

The one telling the story says, "Can you imagine that, can you believe they did that to a man of God?" One of the other musicians says, "What I can't believe is that if he were a man of God, why did God let them do that to him? If he was God's own man, why didn't God bring fire down from heaven and destroy those crackers? That's what I want to know."

Ah, there it is. That's what we'd like to know. Why didn't God step in and nuke those creeps? Why, in fact, does God seem so indifferent to any suffering in this world? Why does he allow rampant injustice? At times, truth to tell, God seems like such an impotent God, an insensitive God. All this misery, innocent children abused, tortured, dying, and God does nothing. Cancer, September 11, war, death, the evil prosper, the wicked climb to the top. The rich get richer and the poor get poorer. And death intrudes into the family. The list is endless.

In the face of so much unfairness there are times we'd like to throttle God, write him off, shake him up, shout at him, if the thought weren't so blasphemous and we weren't so scared. Yet at times we are angry with God or at the very least mightily perplexed, profoundly disappointed, and painfully hurt. Some God. Some divine justice.

I must tell you here in church and quite up front, I have no answers to the misery and unfairness of life and God's terrible silence. I can only offer these three considerations in a long and difficult homily.

First, as far as wicked people go, we say that all we want from God is simple justice. Bring down the dictators, imprison the embezzlers, give payback time to the murderers and cheats, the rapists, and drug dealers. But—be careful what you pray for. Do we, you and I, really want God's absolute justice? Here and now? Think again, because that justice would also come our way as well. Are we ready for that: to be judged strictly, fairly, right down the line? Do we want our every sin judged, our every failing punished, our every connivance, lie, and impurity exposed and punishment meted out? Are second chances to be denied, repentance foreshortened, mercy withheld? Do we really want that when we cry out for justice? It seems rather that when we cry,

"Why doesn't God do something?" we are extremely selective. We really mean why doesn't God do something about *them*? You know, those "others." You know, rain down his justice on those wicked other people. Could it be, though, that God is giving them, even though they cause untold evil and harm, the same chances as ourselves when we cause our own minor brand of evil and harm? Is this seeming indifference a case of extreme divine patience? I don't know.

Second, as far as horrible events go, maybe we just don't see things as God does. In fact, of course, we don't and we can't. God, after all, is mysterious and puzzling. For example, while we're crying out for a just God and the righting of the awful tragedies of life from my retarded child to my spouse's lingering cancer, today's Scripture comes along with some exotic description of God saying of him, "...he shall bring forth justice to the nations"—but, notice—"not crying out, not shouting, not making his voice heard in the street. [Rather] a bruised reed he shall not break and a smoldering wick he shall not quench."

What is this? We *want* God to cry out and shout and make his voice heard in the street. Can't God see all the pain? But he doesn't. Instead he shows a puzzling sensitivity, an unwillingness to break a bruised reed or snuff out a smoldering wick as long as there is the hope of life. Yes, in the end, as promised in the Scriptures, God will bring forth justice for the nations, but apparently it will be worked out in ways we do not understand, because the God of the Bible has an inexplicably soft spot that seems to let this suffering go on in the hopes that the wick of human decency and kindness will flame again.

Third, it would seem—and this is a bold thought indeed—that in all of the overwhelming evil in the world, all the endless suffering, somehow God himself mysteriously seems to suffer along with us. We get the distinct impression that he is not abstracted from our hurts, not apart, looking on like some impotent spectator above it all, not distant from human suffering, but right in the middle of it. It would seem that, ever since God created us, identified with us by making us into his own image and likeness, and then coming into our flesh in the incarnation and taking on our human condition, he mysteriously suffers with us like any passionate lover, like a mother who echoes every hurt of her child in her heart. He throbs with our pain.

You get a sense of that in Elie Weisel's harrowing book *Night*, the story of life and death in a Nazi concentration camp. In one scene, in a reprisal for some misdemeanor the Nazis decided to teach a lesson by hanging three people, including a young boy. Elie Wiesel describes the terrible scene:

> The SS seemed more preoccupied, more disturbed than usual. To hang a young boy in front of thousands of spectators was no light matter.
>
> The head of the camp read the verdict. All eyes were on the child. He was lividly pale, almost calm, biting his lips. The gallows threw its shadow over him....The three victims mounted together onto the chairs. The three necks were placed at the same moment within the nooses. "Long live liberty!" cried the two adults. But the child was silent.
>
> "Where is God? Where is He?" someone behind me asked....The two adults were no longer alive but the third rope was still moving. Behind me I heard the same man asking: "Where is God now?" And I heard a voice within me answer him: "Where is He? There He is. He is hanging here on this gallows."

Can that be? Is somehow God not apart from human suffering but a part of it, still groaning with the pains of giving birth to a people who will do his will? Is it really true what faith says: God in a stinking manger, God crying out in despair in Gethsemane, "Father let this pass me by," and asking on Calvary our oft-asked question, "My God, my God, why have you forsaken me?" Is this God who is also hurting, beseeching, suffering, and dying? Is this God on the gallows of our lives?

But if God is suffering with us, then the next question that comes to mind is this: Is not his rising an answer? Is the resurrection, his resurrection, a sign, a foreshadowing, that God's ultimate justice will triumph when he makes, as he promised, all things new again? If, like any lover, he suffered our agony, cried and died with us, is his resurrection the final response to life's long history of unfairness and senseless pain? Does his resurrection become a sign, a hope, a promise that justice will finally be done, even though meanwhile we have to live with the anger, the puzzlement over the world's seemingly endless pain and suffering?

There is a story about the ancient rabbi Baal Shem-Tov and it goes like this. One day, the rabbi and his students were standing on a hill when they noticed foreign troops invading their town. From their vantage point on the hill they were able to see all the horror and violence of the attack. The rabbi looked up to heaven and cried out, "Oh, if only I were God." A student asked, "But, Master, if you were God, what would you do differently?" The rabbi answered him, "If I were God, I would do nothing differently. But if I were God, I would understand."

We're not God. We do not understand. All that we're left with—and it is much indeed—is Jesus' final act of hope prayed to his Father on our behalf, "Father, into you hands I commend my spirit," and Jesus' final act of vindication from his Father, the resurrection. The one says that God is somehow in the world's senseless pain. The other says that God will redeem it. Perhaps not a very satisfying answer, but it will have to do for now.